HATE AND WAR

HATE AND WAR
THE COLUMN OF MARCUS AURELIUS

IAIN FERRIS

To my sister Judith Ferris

First published 2009

The History Press
The Mill, Brimscombe Port
Stroud, Gloucestershire, GL5 2QG
www.thehistorypress.co.uk

British Library Cataloguing in Publication Data.
A catalogue record for this book is available from the British Library.

ISBN 978 0 7524 4695 0

Typesetting and origination by The History Press
Printed in Great Britain

Contents

Acknowledgements

Thanks and acknowledgement are due to a large number of individuals and organisations for various kinds of help and encouragement in writing this book. Above and beyond the call of duty, my colleague and wife Dr Lynne Bevan read and commented on a draft of the book, much to the benefit of the finished work.

At Tempus Publishing I would like to thank Peter Kemmis Betty, for commissioning this book in the first place, and his successors at The History Press Wendy Logue, Miranda Embleton-Smith and Fran Cantillion for their interest and for editorial advice.

The staff of the Institute of Classical Studies Library, London, the British Library, London and the Special Collections section of the University of Birmingham Library were unfailingly helpful in obtaining books and journals.

For provision of photographs I would like to thank Graham Norrie in particular for producing the many excellent prints of the scenes on the Column of Marcus Aurelius. Thanks are also due to: Daria Lanzuolo of the *Deutsches Archäologisches Institut-Rom* (DAIR) for providing a number of photographic prints for the book; Dr Peter Guest for providing slides of the images of coin portraits of the Antonine dynasty; Dr Tibor Kemenczei, Head of the Archaeology Department, *Magyar Nemzeti Múzeum*, Budapest for providing a photographic print of the Septimus tombstone in the museum's collections; to Dr Fraser Hunter of the National Museums of Scotland, Edinburgh for the photograph of the Bridgeness distance slab; to Tess Watts of the Mary Evans Picture Library for providing the image of the Angel of Mons; to Dr Hélène Walter, who I have been unable to contact, for her illustration of the *Porte Noire* at Besançon; to Dr Penelope Davies for permission to reproduce her plan of the setting of the column; and to the staff of the picture library at the Tate Gallery, London for providing the print of Mark Gertler's *The Merry-Go-Round* and to Luke Gertler for permission to reproduce the picture.

Chapter Five of this book, 'The Scream', first appeared as the core of an article entitled 'Suffering in Silence: the Political Aesthetics of Pain in Antonine Art' in 2006 in 'Past Tense. Studies in the Archaeology of Conflict', Volume One of the *Journal of Conflict Archaeology*. I am grateful to Brill publishers and Dr Tony Pollard and Dr Iain Banks, editors of the *Journal of Conflict Archaeology*, for their kind permission to use this article here in this way.

Finally, for her forebearance, I must thank my wife, Lynne Bevan. I dedicated my previous book to Lynne, so I hope she will not mind that this one is dedicated to my sister Judith.

Picture Credits

Author: 2, 15, 18, 19, 20, 21, 31, 32, 40, 41 and 55; *Deutsches Archäologisches Institut-Rom*: 16, 30, 70 and 73 ; Graham Norrie: 7, 8, 9, 12, 17, 24, 25, 26, 27, 28, 29, 33, 34, 37, 38, 43, 45, 46, 47, 48, 49, 50, 51, 52, 53, 54, 56, 57, 58, 59, 60, 61, 62, 63, 64, 66, 67, 68, 69, 71, 72, 74, 75, 76, 77, 78, 79, 80, 81, 82, 83, 84 and 85; Dr Peter Guest: 1, 3, 4, 5 and 6; Professor Sheppard Frere: 22 and 23; Dr Penelope Davies: 14; Dr Hélène Walter: 35; Mary Evans Picture Library: 36; Tate London: 42; National Museums of Scotland, Edinburgh: 65; Mark Breedon: 44; *Magyar Nemzeti Múzeum*, Budapest: 39.

List of Plates

61 The sacking of a German village. Scene xx. The Column of Marcus Aurelius, Rome. (Photo: Graham Norrie, after Petersen *et al.* 1896).

62 Barbarian male prisoners. Scene LXXVII. The Column of Marcus Aurelius, Rome. (Photo: Graham Norrie, after Petersen *et al.* 1896).

63 A frantic battle and a pile of barbarian bodies. Scene CIX. The Column of Marcus Aurelius, Rome. (Photo: Graham Norrie, after Petersen *et al.* 1896).

64 Mass executions. Scene LXI. The Column of Marcus Aurelius, Rome. (Photo: Graham Norrie, after Petersen *et al.* 1896).

65 The Bridgeness legionary distance slab. (Photo: copyright National Museums of Scotland, Edinburgh).

66 Battle outside a barbarian stronghold. Scene xx. The Column of Marcus Aurelius, Rome. (Photo: Graham Norrie, after Petersen *et al.* 1896).

67 Battle scene, with Roman soldiers crossing a river in boats. Scene XXXIV. The Column of Marcus Aurelius, Rome. (Photo: Graham Norrie, after Petersen *et al.* 1896).

68 Spearing of a barbarian man. Scene LXIII. The Column of Marcus Aurelius, Rome. (Photo: Graham Norrie, after Petersen *et al.* 1896).

69 Spearing of a barbarian man. Scene LXVII. The Column of Marcus Aurelius, Rome. (Photo: Graham Norrie, after Petersen *et al.* 1896).

70 The Portonaccio sarcophagus; Museo Nazionale delle Terme, Rome. (Photo DAIR 61.1399).

71 Roman soldiers dig ditches. Scene XCVIII. The Column of Marcus Aurelius, Rome. (Photo: Graham Norrie, after Petersen *et al.* 1896).

72 Roman soldiers engaged in building activity. Scene LXXXII. The Column of Marcus Aurelius, Rome. (Photo: Graham Norrie, after Petersen *et al.* 1896).

73 Simple huts in a German village being burned by Roman troops. Scene CII. The Column of Marcus Aurelius, Rome. (Photo: DAIR 55.1143).

74 Romanised buildings along the Danube and within the empire. Scene I. The Column of Marcus Aurelius, Rome. (Photo: Graham Norrie, after Petersen *et al.* 1896).

75 A *testudo* engaged in fighting. Scene LIV. The Column of Marcus Aurelius, Rome. (Photo: Graham Norrie, after Petersen *et al.* 1896).

76 Roman cavalry wheel around and form up. Scene CIII. The Column of Marcus Aurelius, Rome. (Photo: Graham Norrie, after Petersen *et al.* 1896).

77 A severed head of a barbarian is presented to the emperor. Scene LXVI. The Column of Marcus Aurelius, Rome. (Photo: Graham Norrie, after Petersen *et al.* 1896).

78 Barbarian prisoners, one of whom is possibly being decapitated in the background. Scene LXIV/LXV. The Column of Marcus Aurelius, Rome. (Photo: Graham Norrie, after Petersen *et al.* 1896).

79 Marcus on the Danube bridge. Scene LXXVIII. The Column of Marcus Aurelius, Rome. (Photo: Graham Norrie, after Petersen *et al.* 1896).

Preface

The Column of Marcus Aurelius in Piazza Colonna in Rome is one of the best-preserved and most significant Roman imperial monuments to have survived in the city. The column was commissioned by Marcus's son Commodus shortly after his father's death in AD 180 and was probably completed in, or shortly before, AD 192. Standing to roughly the same height as the more famous Trajan's Column in Rome, its shaft was decorated with a spiral or helical frieze commemorating Marcus's military campaigns against the *Marcomanni* and other tribes in AD 172–173 and the Sarmatians in AD 174–175 during the First Germanic War. The original column base no longer survives, though drawings of its sculptural programme survive from the Renaissance, while the bronze statue of the emperor that once stood on top of the monument was also probably removed at this time.

The decorated frieze on the shaft of the Column of Marcus Aurelius depicts some of the most graphically violent and harrowing scenes of warfare known from the Roman world and, indeed from the ancient world in general. It is analysis of the nature of these violent scenes of military campaigning depicted on the frieze that must lead any reading of the Column of Marcus Aurelius, though the column cannot, and should not, be read as a literal, chronological commentary on the wars conducted by the emperor. In the numerous battle scenes on the column, many more than appeared on Trajan's Column, there is often almost a sense of panic and frantic endeavour discernible on the part of the Roman forces that seems to be at odds with the almost clinical nature of many of the military manoeuvres depicted on Trajan's Column. While the composition and style of the Trajanic column's battles suggest a sense of order, stressed by the general uniformity of many of the figures of massed troops, on the Aurelian column disharmonic forms and awkward figural poses together create almost the opposite effect. It is difficult to believe that the second-century Roman viewers of the two columns would not have clearly distinguished between the offensive nature of Trajan's expansionist Dacian wars and the defensive, desperate nature of Marcus Aurelius's wars.

The reigns of the emperors Marcus Aurelius and Commodus marked a turning point in the history of the Roman Empire, both in military and cultural terms. The increasing dehumanisation of the barbarian represented in Roman imperial art and reflected in the violent responses of Roman troops on Marcus's column dates from this time and perhaps reflects a deep-seated psychological fear of the barbarian peoples whose incursions over the frontiers of the western empire became the defining events of the empire's final decades. These incursions really were like a river bursting its banks, as they were described at the time by Ammianus Marcellinus.[1]

In the last decade or so much has been written about the relationship between Roman art and Roman imperial policy, indeed about the so-called power of images to virtually define a particular emperor's reign, about the complex interplay between Roman art and state propaganda, and about the role of different kinds of viewer in consuming and interpreting Roman art. It is now universally recognised that there was a difference between the motives and expectations of the creators and patrons of imperial art and the perceptions and understanding of its multiple viewers. The extensive use of images of extreme violence and of suffering barbarian peoples on the Column of Marcus Aurelius and the general use of less violent, more anodyne and stereotypical images of barbarians in the narrative and rhetoric of Roman imperial art elsewhere is an area of study where such a dichotomy can be identified, and where the investigation of the creation and use of stereotypical images of non-Roman peoples penetrates to the very core of the Roman imperial mentality.

This book is not intended to be an in-depth study of the Marcomannic wars of Marcus Aurelius as they relate to Marcus's column or of various barbarian peoples in conflict with the Roman state during his reign. Rather it is an introduction to the study of the column and to how it may have been viewed through contemporary Roman eyes and how the column has been interpreted by generations of scholars since. There will be no attempt to deal in any detail with the history of the wars or with the customs, appearance or material culture of the barbarians depicted on the column frieze; rather the column will be discussed thematically, almost as the series of fractured images it would have appeared to be to a contemporary Roman viewer.

The book consists of nine chapters. Chapter One is an introductory chapter on the reign of Marcus Aurelius and on the form and nature of the column, with a consideration of its setting and design and of the decorated spiral frieze. This chapter also includes some discussion of how the column has been studied by previous generations of scholars. Chapter Two presents an examination of Trajan's Column, the undoubted model for the column of Marcus, and of other monuments of Trajan's reign whose study provides some insights into Roman-barbarian relationships as expressed through Roman imperial art and propaganda. Chapter Three concerns the image of Marcus as it was presented to viewers in the column frieze and questions whether this posthumous image, created under the auspices of his son Commodus some years after his father's death, chimes with other images of Marcus created in his own lifetime and probably with his official sanction.

Chapter Four concentrates on describing and discussing two of the most extraordinary images on the column, the so-called 'Weather Miracles', and on examining the historical background to these events and their significance as both pagan and Christian religious icons. In Chapter Five another of the more iconic images on the column, the image of a screaming man, is discussed in detail, along with an examination of how the viewer's generally empathetic response to this image of suffering may be conditioned by emotional rather than rational reactions. The unusual image of an eroticised Victory and the depiction of mortal barbarian women and their children on the column is examined in Chapter Six, in terms of what these images might tell us about gender relations in contemporary Roman society and about the link between power and sexual dominance. In Chapter Seven the numerous battle scenes on the column will be discussed in the context of the use of violent imagery in Roman society in general and the place of violence more broadly in Roman culture. In Chapter Eight a small number of other individual scenes are examined from the point of view of their visibility to the Roman viewer and their complex iconography, mainly related to the stressing of difference between Roman and non-Roman peoples and their material culture. In the final chapter, Chapter Nine, the artwork of the column is set in its broader political, artistic and cultural context. Academic footnotes and a full bibliography then follow.

It is hoped that this book will act as introduction to the Column of Marcus Aurelius for the informed lay reader interested in the ancient world in general, as well as for undergraduate students of archaeology and art history. The provision of basic academic notes and a full bibliography should allow those wishing to pursue in more depth the more complex and theoretical aspects of the study beyond the book's main narrative to do so with relative ease.

Remarkably, there is no accessible book-length study of the Column of Marcus Aurelius available in English, in contrast to the ready availability of several books on Trajan's Column. There have, however, been numerous articles on the column published in academic journals and in a recent, largely French language volume dedicated to the column, while discussion of the column appears regularly in more general books on Roman art. This present book will hopefully therefore fill an evident gap in the market.

I.M. Ferris
Birmingham, July 2007–September 2008

Meditations on War

The future emperor Marcus Aurelius was born in Rome in AD 121, during the reign of the emperor Hadrian, and died in his late fifties in AD 180 at *Vindobona* – Vienna – while on campaign with the army. He reigned as emperor (*1*) for nineteen years, from AD 161 to AD 180, for part of that time as co-emperor with Lucius Verus and for the last three years of his life as co-emperor with his own son Commodus.

The story of Marcus's life might at first sight seem both extraordinary and ironic, in that this by all accounts most contemplative of men, the author of the Stoic philosophical work known today as the *Meditations*, spent most of his life in training in Rome to rule an empire from its centre and yet spent most of his actual time as emperor away from Rome fighting desperate defensive wars on and beyond her frontiers. In order to understand, or rather to try to understand, the messages intended to be conveyed by the monument known to us today as the Column of Marcus Aurelius (*2*) it will be necessary to first review Marcus's life story as it has come down to us in a number of ancient historical accounts.

In reading ancient written sources one must be aware of the nature of these sources, and sometimes temper reading with suspicion or doubt at the story being presented as historical fact. Who wrote a particular work? Why did they write it and under whose sponsorship? When did they write it relative to the lifetime of the individuals and of the events being described? Can we accept all of the work as true, only some of it, or, indeed, any of it? Why is one particular individual praised and another damned? Has the text subsequently been altered or edited? And so on. There will always be these questions and many others to ask before an ancient text can be used as evidence in some way.

Yet the unreliable narrator does not only lurk in the pages of ancient manuscripts; he or, less likely, she can also be found behind the creation of some of the visual images from the ancient world and in particular from ancient imperial Rome where art and propaganda were inextricably linked. Just as Marcus Aurelius's biographers in some way controlled the versions of his life story on which we rely today for information, so too does the Column of Marcus Aurelius provide a *Res Gestae* for the emperor prepared for public edification by someone other than the person being celebrated. In the case of the Aurelian column it was Marcus's

1 Coin portrait of Marcus Aurelius. (Photo: Peter Guest)

2 A general view of the Column of Marcus Aurelius today, Piazza Colonna, Rome. (Photo: Author)

son Commodus who was responsible for initiating plans for the column, appointing its architect/designer and the artists who would work on its elaborate programme of decoration, approving designs and artwork, financing the scheme, keeping track of progress on site, overseeing the eventual dedication ceremony, and it was he who would bask in the inevitable acclaim accorded this monument, presenting a son's version of how he wished his father's life to seen by audiences in Rome.

In order to begin the exploration of these themes, in this chapter a brief historical account will be given of the reign of Marcus Aurelius, followed by a descriptive analysis of the form and nature of the column set up by Commodus, with a consideration of its setting and design and of the decorated spiral frieze. The opportunity will also be taken to discuss how the column has been studied by previous generations of scholars and to ask whether each generation of art historians and archaeologists has created accounts of the column somehow influenced, in part or in whole, by the major cultural, political and theoretical concerns of their own day.

A life of meditation

Born Marcus Annius Verus in Rome in AD 121, the future emperor Marcus Aurelius led a privileged and cosseted life in a well-connected patrician family related to the families of both the emperors Trajan and Hadrian, though a life not without its sorrows.[1] His father died when Marcus was very young and he was then formally adopted by his grandfather and brought up on the Caelian Hill in Rome. His mother did not remarry. As was normal practice for the patrician class, Marcus was destined to enter into an arranged, strategic marriage and was therefore betrothed to Ceionia Fabia, daughter of the influential Ceionius Commodus, when he was only about fourteen years of age, in either AD 135 or 136, probably because Marcus had already attracted the attention of the emperor Hadrian. This betrothal, though, was to be broken off only a few years later, in AD 138 or 139, to be replaced by an even more strategically important and politically significant marriage alliance linked to the highly complex system of adoption then prevalent among the imperial household and those of the most powerful and influential patrician families in Rome.

Ceionius Commodus was adopted by the emperor Hadrian as his son and heir in or around AD 136, an event that almost overnight introduced the young Marcus formally into the imperial circle. However, Ceionius Commodus died in AD 137 and Hadrian then went on to adopt Aurelius Antoninus as his replacement heir in AD 138 and he, in turn, adopted Marcus, his nephew, and Lucius Commodus. The boys' names now became respectively Marcus Aelius Aurelius Verus and Lucius Aelius Aurelius Commodus. After Hadrian's death and Aurelius Antoninus's succession as the emperor Antoninus Pius in AD 138 (3), the price to pay for Marcus's advancement was his agreement to annul his earlier engagement and instead to become betrothed to the emperor's daughter Annia

3 Coin portrait of Antoninus Pius. (Photo: Peter Guest)

4 Coin portrait of Faustina the Younger. (Photo: Peter Guest)

5 Coin portrait of Faustina the Elder. (Photo: Peter Guest)

Galeria Faustina, Marcus's cousin (*4*). She is generally known to us as Faustina the Younger in order to distinguish her from her mother, Faustina the Elder (*5*), wife of Antoninus Pius. Marcus at the time of his second betrothal was seventeen or eighteen years old; Faustina was eight or nine. Their eventual marriage took place in AD 145, an event commemorated on a number of coin issues.

From AD 138 onwards Marcus's life became that of a leading career politician being groomed for the imperial throne; in AD 138 he was designated *quaestor*, in AD 139 he became a member of the priestly colleges, imperial power and the state religion being symbiotically entwined, and in AD 140 he was appointed consul for the first time, at the same time taking the title 'Caesar' that he was to hold until Antoninus Pius's death in AD 161. He held a second consulship in AD 145.

In AD 147 Faustina gave birth to their first child, a daughter named Domitia Faustina. They would go on to have thirteen or more children – the exact number is not known – and of the seven sons only Commodus survived past infancy.

With the death of Antoninus Pius in AD 161 Marcus assumed power alongside his adopted brother who was now styled as Lucius Verus (*6*). Marcus's reign as emperor was dominated by military matters almost from the very start. There was trouble in Britain, and Parthians and Germans created more severe problems on

6 Coin portrait of Lucius Verus. (Photo: Peter Guest)

the frontiers. In the east the Parthian king Vologases III had seized Armenia and massacred a Roman legion, while in the west the tribe of the *Chatti* had crossed the *limes* and invaded Upper Germany and Raetia. Given the twenty-three years before his accession at the age of forty during which Marcus had gained perhaps the most thorough grounding in politics and the affairs of state of any Roman emperor up to this time, the most remarkable fact to consider about him was that he had never travelled outside of Italy, nor had he gained any meaningful experience in military matters.

It is perhaps therefore not surprising that it was Lucius Verus who went to the Parthian war and could take the credit for capturing the Armenian capital of Artaxata in AD 163 and invading Parthia itself in AD 166 and capturing its capital Ctesiphon. He was granted a triumph for his eastern victories in October AD 166, the first triumph celebrated in Rome for over fifty years. However, in late AD 166 or early AD 167 further trouble erupted elsewhere in the empire, with thousands of *Langobardi* and *Obii* invading *Pannonia*, though they were quickly repulsed, and more minor trouble in Dacia. Marcus and Lucius's expeditions against these barbarian incursions were delayed by what would appear to have been a serious outbreak of plague at Rome, perhaps brought back to the city by Verus's troops returning from the east. In the spring of AD 168 both Lucius and Marcus set out to travel north to where the *Marcomanni* and *Victuali* were causing problems on the frontier. At the age of forty-seven this was Marcus's first journey outside of Italy and Lucius's last. Their negotiations with the troublesome barbarian tribes and inspection of the frontier works and their strengthening were deemed temporarily successful and they returned to Italy early in AD 169. Lucius died on the way back to Rome; he did not reach forty years of age.

If Marcus had found his first military campaign taxing, then what was to come in the next few years would try his lack of battle experience and his patience to the limit. Between AD 170 and his death in AD 180 he spent most of his time on campaign, yet at the same time dedicated himself to the writing of his philosophical work the *Meditations*.

Historians divide up these wars into two major events, called the First Germanic or Marcomannic War which dates from AD 170 to AD 175 and the Second Germanic War from AD 177 to AD 180. While it is not intended here to provide a blow-by-blow account of these wars, for the decorated frieze on the Column of Marcus Aurelius was not intended to be read as a literal, chronological, historical, narrative account of these wars, the main events will now be outlined in summary and then some attempt will be made to see if any the scenes on the column do perhaps marry with historically-attested events.

Marcus returned north alone in the autumn of AD 169. The First War began with a major Roman offensive across the River Danube in the spring of AD 170 which, rather than driving the enemy into retreat, seems to have backfired somewhat and led to the tribes of the *Quadi* and *Marcomanni* invading parts of northern Italy, perhaps reaching as far as the city and port of Aquilea. At the same time the *Costoboci* tribe invaded Macedonia and reached Eleusis. The invaders in northern Italy were quite easily repulsed and Marcus established a new military command structure for Dacia and Upper Moesia. The next year, AD 171, Marcus was stationed at *Carnuntum* in *Pannonia* and there he sought peace with the *Quadi* and at the same time made plans for a major offensive against the more powerful and troublesome *Marcomanni*. This offensive was launched in AD 172 and victory was achieved; Marcus was subsequently awarded the title *Germanicus* in recognition of this victory. Despite previously having sought peace with the *Quadi*, Marcus now attacked them too. It was during this campaign that historians record what are presented as almost supernatural occurrences of thunder and lightening and accompanying heavy rains; these events, known respectively as the 'Miracle of the Thunderbolt' and the 'Miracle of the Rains', will be discussed in detail in Chapter Four below. A treaty was now made with the *Marcomanni* in an attempt to prohibit them from reforming against Rome, the tribe also agreeing to hand over hostages and precious booty, to trade under the auspices of Roman control, and to stay away from a five mile zone along the River Danube.

The next three years saw minor engagements only with the Germanic tribes in AD 173, more serious and extended fighting against the *Quadi* in AD 174 and against the *Iazyges* in the same year, this latter war being particularly savage and uncompromising by all accounts. In AD 175 Marcus launched an assault on the Sarmatians and sued for peace with the *Iazyges*, perhaps more out of necessity since trouble was occurring in the east where the governor of Syria had proclaimed himself emperor in an attempt to usurp Marcus. Marcus returned to Rome.

The Second Germanic War of AD 177 to AD 180 is less well recorded by historians and though again centred on the territories along the upper and middle reaches of the Danube many specific details of the campaigns are missing from their accounts. It would appear that despite the various peace treaties previously signed with the major tribes of the region, trouble resumed here again in AD 177, manifested in the form of small-scale incursions and regular skirmishes with Roman forces. In August of AD 178 Marcus and his son Commodus, who was now co-emperor, set out from Rome to the war zone. In the next year a victory is recorded, possibly over the *Quadi*. In AD 180 new field campaigns were planned but on March 17th Marcus died at *Vindobona* – Vienna – before the fighting began. He was fifty-eight years old.

Many commentators see certain phenomena emerging during the reign of Marcus which were to become more pronounced in the following centuries and which might be seen as being symptomatic of the crises which were eventually to engulf the Roman empire, that is constant trouble and pressure on the frontiers and mass barbarian incursions into the empire often caused by mass migrations of people from beyond the frontiers. The historian Dio Cassius, commenting on the accession of Commodus, wrote that, 'our history now descends from a kingdom of gold to one of iron and rust, as affairs did for the Romans of that day'.[2] Commodus may have spent an inordinate amount of money on gladiatorial games but he left little physical impact on the fabric of the city, the column dedicated to his parents and a temple dedicated to Jupiter within the Palatine palace being the only major building projects that he is known to have sponsored.

We know a great deal about Marcus's innermost thoughts and feelings from his personal notebooks – now known as the *Meditations* – which he kept for the last decade or so of his life. Marcus is therefore virtually alone of the later Roman emperors in leaving some personal record of his life to provide sometimes much-needed contrast to the accounts of often-biased historians. However, as has been pointed out by Anthony Birley, author of the definitive modern biography of Marcus, there are some, 'who view the *Meditations* as the musings of a self-conscious prig'.[3] These notebooks, though, tell us little or nothing about the affairs of the Roman state, nor, perhaps surprisingly, do they allude much to Marcus's wars, even though most of the work was written while he was on campaign among the *Quadi* or at the major military base at *Carnuntum*. They are, however, though concerned to a very great and obvious degree with thoughts of death.

The *Meditations* are divided into twelve books or chapters, the first of which allows Marcus to look back on the great, positive influences of his early life, including his friends, his family and his teachers, first among the latter being his tutor Marcus Cornelius Fronto. In the other books, in the words of Anthony Birley, Marcus was seeking, 'to remind himself, while far from home, in difficult and often exhausting circumstances, of the lessons he had learned in happier times'.[4]

Given that the present study, written some eighteen hundred years after Marcus's death, is trying to interpret the monumental remains related to Marcus's life, it is ironic that in the *Meditations* he constantly mused on what he saw as the fleet passing of posthumous fame:

> Well, then, shall mere glory distract you? Look at the swiftness of the oblivion of all men; the gulf of endless time, behind and before; the hollowness of applause, the fickleness and folly of those who seem to speak well of you, and the narrow room in which it is confined. This should make you pause. For the entire earth is a point in space, and how small a corner thereof is this your dwelling place, and how few and how paltry those who will sing your praises here.[5]

In a number of passages in the *Meditations* Marcus dwells on images of the human body and its frailty, and a number of these are worth quoting here for the light they shed on Marcus's possible mindset during these hard years on campaign. In the first passage Marcus considers the human body, 'Distain the flesh: blood and bones and network, a twisted skein of nerves, veins, arteries'.[6] In the second he considers the body ravaged by the effects of war, 'If you have ever seen a dismembered hand or foot or a head cut off, lying somewhere apart from the rest of the trunk, you have an image of what a man makes of himself'.[7] Finally, at one stage he depressingly wonders, 'how does the ground have room for the bodies of those who for so long an age are buried in it?'[8] This severe morbidity is perhaps almost a symptom of battle fatigue and post-traumatic stress disorder.

The hundred-footer

The Column of Marcus Aurelius is almost exactly one hundred feet tall (29.6 metres), measuring the height of the Doric column itself, with the overall monument being thirty nine metres in height.[9] The fourth-century Regionary Catalogues record the height of the monument as one hundred and seventy five and a half Roman feet, equivalent to 51.95 metres, a discrepancy which can probably be accounted for by the ancient measurement including the height of the statue or statues that stood on top of the column and the original height of the base and pedestal down to the ancient contemporary ground surface, which Amanda Claridge has calculated is probably almost seven metres below the present-day ground surface of Piazza Colonna.[10]

The column shaft is a straight cylinder only one hundred and forty millimetres narrower at the top than at the bottom, resting upon an oak-leaf ornament. The twenty-six drums of Luna marble forming the column shaft were originally held together by iron dowels, many of which have decayed or been robbed-out, leaving some of the drums to shift, producing some kinks in the line of the shaft. The monument was built of fine white Italian Luna marble, though it has subsequently been repaired with other materials, most extensively the coarser, greyish white Proconnesian marble used in the sixteenth-century programme of repair works.

The original base of the column was much eroded and damaged before its necessary replacement in 1589 (7). The present doorway into the base is in the south side, whereas it had originally been in the east side (8). The column has an internal spiral staircase of two hundred steps up to a viewing platform on the top. The staircase is lit by a series of rectangular slit windows which on the outside have been skilfully integrated into the scenes decorating the frieze. There are thirty-nine windows in the shaft and there were probably originally forty-five windows in total, including those lighting the interior of the original base. The door at the top which opens onto the viewing platform is set in the north-west angle of the platform, a choice of position dictated perhaps both by safety concerns and by the door's specific opening alignment, a probably deliberate design detail which will be discussed further below. Access into the base and up the staircase was likely to have always been restricted by the monument's full-time custodian.

In comparison with Trajan's Column, the number of spiral bands on the

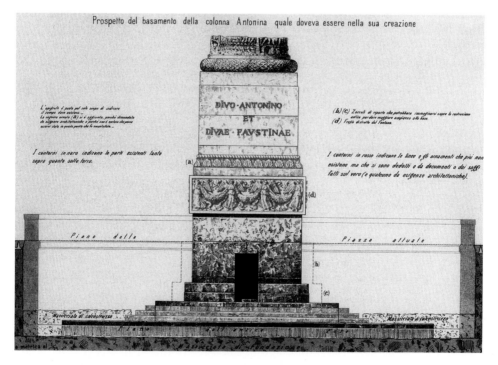

7 Reconstruction drawing of the base of the Column of Marcus Aurelius, Rome.
(Photo: Graham Norrie, after Petersen *et al.* 1896)

Column of Marcus Aurelius, onto which a decorated frieze was carved, has been reduced from twenty-two to twenty, the pitch of the helix on Marcus's column is steeper and the actual carving itself is deeper there, creating higher relief, all of these stylistic strategies having been employed to enhance visibility of the images on the frieze. Again, probably for the same reason, the number of individual figures featuring in the action depicted on the frieze on Marcus's column has been cut down and these figures are generally larger in size than those on Trajan's Column. In certain instances visibility of Marcus's column frieze could have been further enhanced by the use of colour or gilding, as is again discussed further below. It is also worth noting that the setting of the column in what was probably an open square also served to enhance its viewing in certain respects. The programmatic organising of certain scenes, particularly those involving Marcus himself, once more would have lent greater clarity to the message of the monument (9). These undoubted improvements in visibility indicate that a prolonged and systematic analysis of the visual failings of the frieze on Trajan's Column had taken place during the design of the Aurelian column.

There has been a great deal of academic discussion over the past decade in particular about the viewing of Roman art; how monuments or artworks were intended to be received by their audience and how this audience of viewers would react to such viewings depending on their own status, knowledge, perceptions

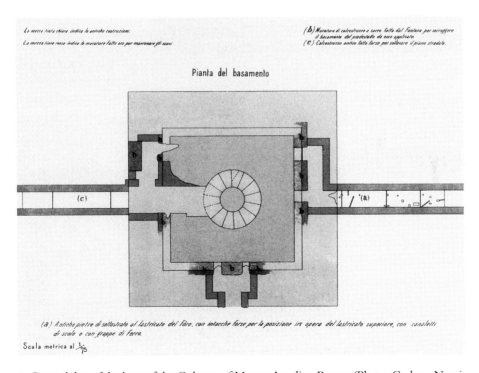

8 Groundplan of the base of the Column of Marcus Aurelius, Rome. (Photo: Graham Norrie, after Petersen *et al.* 1896)

9 The emperor with
the army. Scene CIX.
The Column of Marcus
Aurelius, Rome. (Photo:
Graham Norrie, after
Petersen *et al.* 1896)

or even prejudices. The first point to be made about the friezes around both
Trajan's Column and the Column of Marcus Aurelius is that it would never
have been intended that viewers on the ground would walk round and round
the monuments to follow the narrative on the friezes from the bottom to the
top. If attempting this, even with the scenes being enhanced by painting, clarity
would be lost in viewing scenes on the upper parts of the columns, leaving
aside the dizziness which would inevitably ensue. So how were these friezes to
be viewed?

It would seem that the viewer, once he or she had taken in the overall form
of the monument and its setting, would probably have viewed the monument
selectively. Almost everyone would have been likely to view the lower few spirals
sequentially by walking round the column, perhaps concentrating on one or
two particularly striking scenes or images. Viewing after that would have been
more selective.

A further aid to viewing was probably provided by the painting of the decorative
frieze. The Renaissance rediscovery of Greek and Roman artworks went hand in
hand with a taste for white marble sculptures. For many years the echo of this

effect resulted in the widespread assumption that most ancient sculpture was formed of unadorned stone and bronze. However, the use of paint to varying degrees on ancient works of art to completely cover a sculpture or frieze's surface or to highlight specific details by its sparing use is now well attested but paint seldom survives on most works of art. Marble is by nature an excellent medium on which to paint and its painting can therefore be assumed in many cases. There is a growing interest in the study of the use of ancient painting in this context, most recently manifested in the exhibition 'The Color of Life. Polychromy in Sculpture from Antiquity to the Present' held at the Getty Villa Museum in Malibu, California in 2008.[11]

But would the sculpted friezes on monuments such as Trajan's Column and the Column of Marcus Aurelius have been painted? We will never know for certain, but a general consensus would seem to be that some painting, colouring, highlighting or gilding of parts of the friezes did take place. Certainly some figures on Trajan's Column would have held small metal weapons, again another type of strategy for further improving their visibility. As an illustration of this possibility, a cast of one of the battle scenes (Scene XXXII) from the frieze on Trajan's Column was painted fully under the guidance of the Italian art historian Ranuccio Bianchi Bandinelli for use as a prop in an Italian television programme in 1971. Bianchi Bandinelli has subsequently made use of images of this coloured cast in one of his academic publications.[12] The painted scene is remarkably successful in terms of its subtlety and the way that, in particular, it brings out detail of the protagonists' arms and armour, for example decorated shields and scale armour. The painting would certainly have made the scene visible from further away but there must still have been some kind of cut-off point relating to visibility and distance on both columns. The Italian painted cast is certainly much more subtle in its effects than the painted Parthenon frieze panels imagined depicted by the Victorian artist Sir Lawrence Alma Tadema being inspected *in situ* on scaffolding by Pheidias. In this painting, now in Birmingham Art Gallery, the painted frieze panels are bright and garish, lacking the nuanced subtlety of the Bianchi Bandinelli painted cast.

Certainly as sculptural techniques changed there may consequently have been less use of colour on ancient stone sculpture, 'the increasingly coloristic use of textural effects in the treatment of the hair, and especially in the rendering of the eyes, where shallow drill-holes suggested light glancing off the pupils, implies that late-Roman sculptors began to move away from the tradition of painted statuary altogether'.[13] Whether smaller-scale figures such as those on the column frieze benefitted from such textural effects is debatable.

Recent research by Martin Beckmann and by Amanda Claridge, prompted by Beckmann's work, has thrown some new light on the probable construction methods employed in building the column and in carving the frieze.[14] This work has centred on the analysis of the border of the frieze, an element of the monument which at first sight might not appear worthy of detailed examination but whose close study by Beckmann has thrown up much new information about the way in which the column was built.

The decorated frieze was cut into the outer surface of the marble drums which form the column shaft to a depth of *c.*100 millimetres, a raised border of *c.*70–80 millimetres delineating the upper and lower edges of the frieze. Beckmann has suggested that 'the border was created by being reserved from the stone of the shaft as the carving of the frieze progressed'.[15] A variety of patterns was carved to form the border, including parallel lines of small lumps, 'erratic, jagged, and random patterns, in others brick-like schemes'.[16] Beckmann has plotted the positions of each different type of border carving and has concluded that 'the varied patterns exhibit clear and abrupt breaks between them, and both the patterns and breaks often have clear relationships to the frieze itself'.[17] Border patterns on Trajan's Column had appeared very rock-like and, as such, were intended to form ground surfaces on which some action took place. No such use was made of the borders on the Aurelian column.

Obviously such a great variation in the nature of the carved border suggests that many individuals were engaged in its carving and that this was not necessarily a job for the most skilled craftsmen/artists on the project. Beckmann has suggested that forty-six different carvers worked on the borders, though his subsequent theories of how the workforce operated on site, extrapolated from his plotting of the various border patterns, is less convincing.[18]

Beckmann ended his analysis by making what appears to be the rather obvious assertion that 'the work of carving the frieze was … subordinate to the drafting of its actual content', in other words, that in one case he discusses 'the carvers had a fairly detailed plan of the scene to hand'.[19] A significant project such as this would certainly have had detailed plans and drawings, sketches and roughs ready-prepared for the work, and guide drawings would have been made from these directly onto the stone surfaces of the column shaft. Perhaps this view, implying that one might have expected the construction and adornment of the column to be somehow an *ad hoc* process, is part of the long history of negative analysis of the column. It has certainly not been suggested at all that the frieze on Trajan's Column was created *in situ* in this way by a team of carvers working on their own initiative. Rather, the existence of detailed field drawings contemporary with Trajan's campaigns has been posited, with these drawings forming the basis of illustrated reports on the war submitted by the emperor to the senate in Rome and subsequently utilised as source material for the design of the decorated frieze on Trajan's Column. A similar design process probably occurred during the construction of the Column of Marcus Aurelius.

Beckmann's study did, however, lead to a debate about the way in which the column had been constructed and it was subsequently suggested by Amanda Claridge that the evidence, including Beckmann's analysis of the frieze's border, pointed towards a five-phase construction programme.[20] Firstly, the whole column was erected, including the setting up of the statue or statues on the top, using a lifting tower of some sort that would be gradually reduced in stages as the work programme progressed. Following that, in the second phase of work, the statuary pedestal was finished off, as was the top of the capital. The third phase saw the laying out of the helix for the frieze on the column shaft, plotted against four vertical lines marked out on the four window axes, down the whole length of the shaft. The border pattern was then carved to provide a guiding boundary for the frieze, with the vertical guidelines being retained for the same purpose. In the fourth phase the tower was now totally dismantled and replaced by lighter scaffolding, fixed to the column through the window slits. The carving of the frieze now began, from the bottom upwards, with the scaffolding being raised as work progressed. Once work had reached the top, the scaffolding would have been lowered stage by stage as the final finishes were made to the reliefs and the window frames were carved. The guideline strips were now carved to blend in and the border strips across these lines were joined up. The fifth and final stage saw the column base carvings carried out, the relief panels and the dedicatory inscription either being carved *in situ* or set in place, having been prepared in a workshop off site, and the eagles and garlands carved. The interior of the column base and the insertion of the staircase and so on could have been carried out as part of the works at any stage following the phase one works.

It would take a professional quantity surveyor to work out the hypothetical man days of labour involved in the various stages of the construction programme for the column and the provision of its artworks and there must therefore be scepticism about estimates of the size of the potential labour force that have appeared in print. Suffice it to say, the building and decoration of the column constituted the most labour-intensive imperial building project seen in Rome for decades, a task of apparent filial piety that Commodus must have hoped would earn him credit and popularity with the Roman people.

Antiquarian illustration

The column base as it exists today is a relatively modern construction, as was noted above. The original column base, obviously by then badly damaged, was removed and replaced during the major renovation works on the column in the sixteenth century. Unfortunately, and surprisingly, the original decorated panels from the base were not apparently retained at this time or added to the many collections of Roman antiquities in the city and we therefore have to rely on a number of antiquarian illustrations of the base to aid its reconstruction and in order to interpret the sculptural scenes on it.[21] The decorating of the base of the column, along with the provision of the decorated spiral frieze, linked the monument to the similarly endowed Trajan's Column and not to the Column of Antoninus Pius which had a decorated base but a plain, undecorated, though coloured marble, column shaft.

The antiquarian drawings, however, cannot necessarily be taken at face value as being entirely accurate. Illustrations of two of the four sides of the rectangular base pre-date the major sixteenth-century renovation works and were made by Enea Vico and Francisco d'Hollanda, working more or less at the same time, in 1540 and 1539–1540 respectively. The first drawing, by d'Hollanda (*10*), is of a panel on the northern face of the base, decorated with images of four winged victories standing equidistant from one another and with a long swag or garland draped over their shoulders. The two victories at the centre are placed either side of a slit window and in their outstretched hands each holds a victor's laurel wreath that is held also on the other side by the outer victories. These figures were probably repeated on the southern and western faces of the column base. The second drawing, by Vico (*11*), shows the base's eastern face's decorated panel in which Marcus himself appears, in the company of a number of Roman officers and soldiers, one of these men possibly being Marcus's son Commodus, hearing the pleas of some male barbarian prisoners, two of whom kneel at the emperor's feet in supplication. At one end of the panel scene stands a riderless horse, one foreleg raised, perhaps the most enigmatic image in the overall, crowded scene. Both the Vico and the d'Hollanda drawings are simple in their execution and are closer to being sketches than detailed record drawings.

10 D'Hollanda's drawing of 1539/1540 of the original base of the Column of Marcus Aurelius, Rome. (Photo: after Colini 1954 Tav. II)

11 Vico's drawing of 1540 of the original base of
the Column of Marcus Aurelius, Rome. (Photo:
after Colini 1954 Tav. II)

At first sight a drawing of 1762 by Giovanni Battista Piranesi, the renowned
architectural fabulist, showing the eastern face's decorated panel, looks much
more seductively promising, perhaps because of its accomplished style which
seems to speak somehow of definitive authenticity. Here once more we see
Marcus receiving the captured barbarians, the surrounding Roman officers
and the riderless horse. However, if Piranesi's drawing of this scene is compared
with the earlier drawings in which this face of the base is represented,
problems of accuracy are highlighted. Many more background figures appear
in the Piranesi illustration and, most significantly, the panel scene presented
by Piranesi is carved in higher relief and has a crispness missing from the
earlier depictions . Piranesi's prospect for the drawing also allows us to gain a

tantalising glimpse of part of a third face of the base which would appear to be decorated with another crowded scene, maybe also of supplication and *clementia*. However, this is most probably a total invention on his part, as it is generally accepted that scenes with victories holding garlands appeared on three sides of the base.

Neither of these base-panel scenes is out of the ordinary in terms of triumphal Roman imperial imagery and they fit in well with the artworks on the frieze, in content if perhaps not in style, as far as can be judged from the sketch-like sixteenth-century drawings. The friezes echo some of the images on the column: Marcus granting clemency, Victory inscribing details of the war on a shield, and a riderless horse in a depiction of the Roman forces crossing a pontoon bridge over the River Danube.

Attempts have been made to produce reconstruction drawings of the column base as it might originally have been conceived, making use of both the evidence provided by the antiquarian illustrators (*12*), comparison with other monuments in Rome and further afield, and the testimony of archaeological excavation. A reconstruction by Martina Jordan-Ruwe published in 1990, not reproduced here, is almost Piranesian in the allure of its completeness but, when it comes down to it, perhaps equally fantastic.[22] The Vico and d'Hollanda panels are accepted as the most accurate representations of these two scenes and are placed at mid-base height in the reconstruction. Below them is a taller register of decoration comprising a weapons frieze, as is found on the base of Trajan's Column, and above them, on the reconstruction of the eastern face, again in a tall register of the same size as the weapons frieze panel, is a register containing two large winged figures representing victory holding a framed panel for a dedicatory inscription, one victory standing to either side. On a plinth above cornice level are four marble eagles, one at each corner. These eagles could be not only imperial eagles, but they could also represent Jupiter's eagle, thus introducing yet another reference to the pairing of Marcus with Jupiter and to the Miracle of the Thunderbolt, both of which are discussed at length in Chapter Four.

In many respects the column base was the most significant part of the monument in terms of its importance in putting across a message to the viewer about Marcus, about Commodus and about the power of Rome. The decorated areas on the base and, of course, the now-lost inscription there would have been accessible to every viewer, unlike the column shaft's frieze which invited and necessitated different strategies of viewing as will be discussed throughout this volume. The need, therefore, for the base to be simple to read would appear to have been paramount and has resulted in the simplicity of the recurring motifs of the victories with swags and the easy-to-understand scene of imperial *clementia*.

The inscription, we must assume, would have made explicit the role of Commodus in setting up the column and his piety towards his late parents. This statement of filial piety, also made clear in the very monumentality of the column itself, might have been intended to hark back to the time when imperial lineage, guaranteed through the blood line and the family, was seen as a security measure for political stability in Roman affairs, as opposed to the impression of instability in the era of adopted emperors.

Finally, it has been commented upon how similar in general form the drawn base panels are to the long front panels of Roman decorated stone sarcophagi and, indeed, how the composition of the basal frieze scene involving the emperor, kneeling, subservient barbarians and the riderless horse again recalls many frontal compositions on so-called biographical sarcophagi on which such scenes of *clementia* would become almost standard. Further possible links between the style and content of battle scenes on the column frieze and the decoration of Antonine battle sarcophagi, as they are called, are discussed in Chapter Five.

No original dedicatory inscription from the column base was recorded by the antiquarian illustrators of the column before its restoration in the sixteenth century and it must be assumed, therefore, that a panel or panels containing such an inscription were removed long before this time, perhaps even in Roman times following the *damnatio memoriae* of Commodus. However, a lengthy inscription relating to the column has been recovered from nearby and is now in the collections of the Vatican Museums.[23] This inscription was set up in the summer of AD 193 by a freedman of the emperor Septimius Severus called Adrastus who held the position of *procurator* or custodian of the column and in it he records how he applied for permission to build a small custodian's hut nearby on public land so that he could more efficiently carry out his duties on site (*13*). Permission was granted for the construction of the hut the inscription tells us. From the text of the inscription we learn that the monument was known variously as *columna centenaria divorum Marci et Faustinae*, in translation, 'the hundred-foot column of the deified Marcus and Faustina' or *columna centenaria divi Marci*, in translation, 'the hundred-foot column of the Divine Marcus' and even simply as *columna centenaria*, 'the hundred-footer'.

Surviving the centuries

In comparison with some of the other major ancient monuments of Rome, the Column of Marcus Aurelius has survived in a worse state of preservation than, for instance, the nearby Trajan's Column but in a much better state than a monument such as the Arch of Septimius Severus in the forum. The column has suffered from severe weathering, some of it brought about by atmospheric pollution, but it has also, more seriously, been damaged by earthquakes on more than one occasion; it has also been struck by lightning, rather ironically, given that one of the more curious scenes portrayed on the decorated column frieze is the so-called Miracle of the Thunderbolt. Marcus's column has been restored or at least renovated and cleaned on a number of occasions, the most intensive period of works being in the sixteenth century when in 1589 Pope Sixtus V employed Domenico Fontana to almost completely overhaul the decaying monument, many of the repairs being undertaken using marble from

12 Prospect view of
the Column of Marcus
Aurelius and Piazza
Colonna, Rome in the
seventeenth century.
(Photo: Graham Norrie,
after Petersen *et al.* 1896)

the Roman building known as the *Septizodium* at the foot of the Palatine Hill.[24] It was at this time that the remnants of decorative panels on the column base were removed and lost, and a new base constructed. The column was re-dedicated to Saint Paul, whose statue was now set up on top of the monument to act as a pendant to the statue of Saint Peter set up on top of the nearby Trajan's Column.

It is not the purpose of this present study to consider the post-Roman history of the monument in anything other than the most general terms, particularly with regard to listing or attempting to list the many different phases of repair, renovation and conservation that the column has undergone. In any case, such information can be found published in detail elsewhere. Again, with the exception of the consideration of what has been called elsewhere in this volume the Christianisation of the monument, the post-Roman afterlife of the column has not been considered here either. The reception of the column in subsequent eras and its life as part of the very fabric of the city of Rome and of Piazza Colonna up to the present day is a fascinating topic and one which formed the basis of a small exhibition some years ago at Palazzo Braschi and of its accompanying catalogue.[25]

EXEMPLARIA · LITTE
RARVM · RATIONALI
VM · DOMINORVM · NN
SCRIPTARVM · PERTINEN
TES AD · ADRASTVM
AVGG · NN · LIB · QVIBVS · AEI
PERMISSVM · SIT · AEDIFI
CARE · LOCO · CANNABAE
A SOLO · IVRIS SVI · PECVNIA
SVA · PRESTATVRVS · SOLARI
VM · SICVT · CAETERI
AELIVS · ACHILLES · CL · PERPETV
VS · FLAVIANVS · EVTYCHVS
EPAPHRODITO · SVO · SALVTEM
TEGVLAS OMNES · ET · INPENSA
DE CASVLIS · ITEM CANNABIS
ET · AEDIFICIIS · IDONEIS · ADSIGNA
ADRASTO · PROCVRATORI ·
COLVMNAE · DIVI · MARCI · VT
AD VOLVPTATEM · SVAM · HOSPI
TIVM · SIBI · EX · STRVAT · QVOD · VT
HABEAT · SVI · IVRIS · ET · AD HE
REDES · TRANSMITTAT ·
LITTERAE · DATAE · VIII · IDVS
AVG · ROMAE · FALCONE · ET
CLARO · COS
AELIVS · ACHILLES · CL · PERPETV
VS · FLAVIANVS · EVTYCHVS · AQVI
LIO · FELICI · HADRASTO · AVG · LIB
AD AEDIFICIVM · QVOD · CVSTODI
AE · CAVSA · COLVMNAE · CENTE
NARIAE · PECVNIA · SVA · EXSTRVC
TVRVS · EST · TIGNORVM · VEHES
DECEM · QVANTI · FISCO CONSTI
TERVNT · CVM PONTEM · NECES
SE · FVIT · COMPINGI · PETIMVS·
DARI · IVBEAS · LITTERAE · DATAE
XIIII · KAL · SEPT · ROMAE
FALCONE · ET · CLARO · COS
RATIONALES · SEIO · SVPERSTITI
ET · FABIO · MAGNO · PROCVRA
TOR · COLVMNA · CENTENARIAE
DIVI · MARCI · EXSTRVERE · HABI
TATIONEM · IN · CONTERMINIS
LOCIS · IVSSVS · OPVS · ADGREDI
ETVR · SI AVCTORITATEM · VES
TRAM · ACCEPERIT · PETIMVS·
IGITVR · AREAM · QVAM · DEMO
NSTRAVERIT · ADRASTVS · LIB
DOMINI · N · ADSIGNARI · EI · IVBEA
TIS · PRAESTATVRO · SECVNDVM
EXEMPLVM · CETERORVM · SO
LARIVM · LITTERAE · DATAE ·
VII · IDVS · SEPT · ROMAE · RED
DITAE · IIII · IDVS · SEPT · ROMAE
ISDEM · COS

13 The Adrastus inscription. (Photo: after CIL 6.1585)

The setting of the column

The setting of the column, its place in the urban fabric of Rome, is of considerable interest and is a matter that has often been forgotten or neglected in studies of the monument. Although the main focus of this book is the column itself and in particular the artworks that adorn it, some consideration will be given here to its formal setting.

The column is in the central part of the *Campus Martius* which lies to the north of the various forums of Rome (*14*). In her important study *Death and the Emperor* the art historian Penelope Davies has analysed the positions of all the imperial funerary monuments in Rome from the time of Augustus up to the erection of Marcus's column.[26] Her description of the ancient setting of the column is worth quoting in full:

> In antiquity, the Column of Marcus Aurelius stood at the center of a precinct similar to the court surrounding Trajan's Column but substantially larger. Nestled between the Via Lata/Flaminia to the east and the Via Recta to the south, the precinct opened on to the Via Flaminia, at a level approximately three meters higher than the road. A monumental arch demarcating the entry may have originally borne the Aurelian panel reliefs some of which were subsequently reused on the Arch of Constantine and others of which are now in the Palazzo dei Conservatori, Rome. Reconstructions place porticoes on the east, north, and south sides of the precinct, and on the west side, under the nineteenth-century Palazzo Wedekind, a Temple to Divine Marcus, featured in the Regionary Catalogues.[27]

The first, perhaps most obvious point to make, is that the Column of Marcus Aurelius is only a relatively short distance away from Trajan's Column, the very monument that inspired both the form of Marcus's column and the style of decoration employed on the later monument. While there would not have been a clear line of sight anywhere between the two monuments at ground level, it is possible, and highly likely, that on those rare occasions when anyone would go to the top of either monument, the other would be visible from that vantage point. Perhaps for centuries the original, now-lost statues that adorned the top of each column could stare across the rooftop cityscape at each other in mute recognition of their subject's individual achievements, successes and failures. While this might sound purely facetious, it must be remembered that statues played an extraordinary role in Roman society and that to position one statue to 'look at' another was not the alien concept it might appear today.[28]

If one considers the mortuary aspects of the two monuments, then this juxtaposition through some sight line, however rarely viewed, seems perhaps deliberate. Marcus's column was also quite close to, and perhaps in the line of sight of, the Column of Antoninus Pius that Marcus himself, along with his sometime co-emperor Lucius Verus, had been instrumental in having erected. This siting was probably not coincidental, nor indeed was the fact that Marcus's column was also, it would seem, part of a complex of Antonine structures and buildings

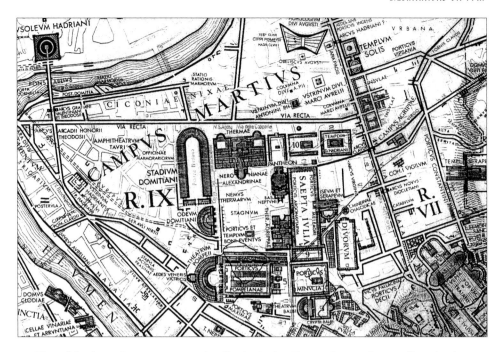

14 Plan of the Antonine commemorative district in the *Campus Martius*, Rome. (Drawing by permission of Penelope Davies)

that included the Temple of *Divus Marcus,* in the forecourt of which the column possibly stood. Just outside the precinct was the Column of Antoninus Pius and three altars, one of which was certainly the *ustrinum* of Antoninus Pius, the two others also probably having links with the Antonine dynasty.[29]

As Penelope Davies has noted 'the Column establishes Marcus Aurelius as the worthy successor of Rome's "good" emperors: of Augustus and the Antonines by manipulation of a viewer's panorama; and of Trajan, *Optimus Princeps,* by the very choice of a sculpted column'.[30] Davies has pointed out that even the placing of the door at the top of Marcus's column which opens onto the viewing platform, set in the north-west angle of the platform, is a choice of position dictated not only by safety concerns but also by the door's specific opening alignment, giving the viewer an immediate vista onto Augustus's and Hadrian's mausolea 'within a single eye-span' as he or she came through the door.[31]

It is now accepted that the correct way to view and interpret the Column of Marcus Aurelius is to classify the monument as a funerary memorial, part of a continuum of monumentalising the memories of the Roman emperors within the urban fabric of Rome itself that began with the mausoleum of Augustus and which was, in fact, to end with this column. This thesis was developed by Penelope Davies who has eloquently argued that there is a danger that by studying individual monuments in isolation we could be 'blurring links between monuments of different types'.[32] All of these monuments are what Davies has dubbed 'accession monuments', part of a chain of imperial myth-making that helped perpetuate the functioning of the state apparatus through monumentality.[33] Davies found that there were quite clear links between the physical siting of imperial funerary monuments and the psychological siting of an emperor's heritage in the Roman continuum of history. The emperors, she convincingly maintained, 'appear to have selected sites to align their monuments with select pre-existing structures, and the alignments seem uniformly to have stressed dynastic ties, both with the emperor's immediate dynasty and with earlier rulers; on the whole, they appear to have been designed to encourage association rather than rivalrous comparison'.[34]

It was in the *Campus Martius* that the cremation of the bodies of the Roman emperors took place, a process that led to divinisation and legitimate accession of the new emperor through observing the rite. Apotheosis was reflected in the subsequent erection of temples and although little is known about the temple of *Divus Marcus* – the Divine Marcus –, despite the fact that it is referred to in literary sources and in the so-called Regionary Catalogues, it most probably stood in a courtyard surrounding the column, again in part of the ancient *Campus Martius*. The column was probably symbolically sited between the Temple of Hadrian and Antoninus Pius's Column. Marcus's ashes, however, were interred in Hadrian's Mausoleum, also the last resting place of the ashes of Lucius Verus. It is of great interest that the ingrained view of the *Campus Martius* as a place of imperial accession, where the affairs of both dead and living emperors merged through monumentality, finds visual expression on the decorated base of the Column of Antoninus Pius. There to witness the depicted apotheosis of Antoninus Pius and his wife Faustina is a male personification of the *Campus Martius*, identifiable by the fact that he holds in his left hand the obelisk of Augustus's sundial, a sure indicator of the power of place in ancient Rome.[35]

A kingdom of iron and rust

In interpreting the Column of Marcus Aurelius as a funerary monument, like the columns of Trajan and Antoninus Pius, rather than a triumphal one, Penelope Davies does not allow for the possibility that it could have been both of these things, according to the motives of Commodus who had the column erected.

The design, building and dedication of the column were all executed by the emperor Commodus in honour of his father Marcus and mother Faustina. The monument should therefore tell us something about Commodus himself, though it cannot be examined in the broader context of other architectural and monument commissions of his reign, as these were few.

Commodus reigned from AD 180 to AD 192, though he had held the imperial throne jointly with Marcus for the three years before his father's death. The portraits of Commodus that survived his *damnatio memoriae* tell us most about the way in which he wished to be seen and perceived by the Roman viewers. These portraits are traditionally divided into five main types,[36] starting with the youthful crown prince, but the most startling single work is the unique portrait of Commodus in the guise of Hercules from the Esquiline Hill and now in the Museo del Palazzo Conservatori in Rome (*15*).[37] The historical accounts tell us that the emperor became increasingly obsessed with Hercules and would dress in a manner similar to that seen in the portrait, his head draped with a lion's skin, a club in his hand. Believing himself to be a manifestation of the god, the emperor even vowed to appear to fight in the Colosseum arena to demonstrate his power and divinity. His assassination took place before Romans could be subjected to this delusional spectacle. It is possible that Commodus adopted the persona of Hercules, the divine son of Jupiter (Zeus) in order to stress his direct blood ties with his father. Jupiter was the god with whom Marcus Aurelius was most closley identified through the Weather Miracles, as will be discussed in detail in Chapter Four.

To return to the portrait bust, however, Commodus is not only attired in the guise of Hercules but he appears bare chested. As well as holding a knobbed club over his right shoulder, he holds some apples in his left hand, doubtless representing the golden apples of the Hesperides. The lion skin is tied in a knot beneath his chin, the clawed paws of the great Nemean beast hanging down on his chest, its upper set of mighty teeth seemingly hovering above the emperor's curly hair. The bust is set on a *pelta* above crossed *cornucopiae* and an orb. The small figure of a now-headless amazon kneels to one side of the base.

It has been suggested that this bust was displayed in some public place, in which case one wonders about the viewer's reaction to such a bizarre and theatrical work of art. Whatever cachet Commodus might have gained through the honouring of his parents by the erection of the column to their memory was probably soon lost through his reported delusional behaviour. Perhaps Commodus's desire to commemorate his dead father in such a grandiose manner, with the most elaborate and labour-intensive programme of artworks since the time of Trajan, in the form of the frieze on the column, arose from some element of guilt over his rumoured involvement in the alleged poisoning of Marcus.

At first sight, it is perhaps surprising that the Column of Marcus Aurelius was not depicted on any Roman coin issues, as so often happened with the major monuments of Rome. Indeed, coins often provide information about the existence or form of lost monuments in Rome. Both Trajan's Column and the Column of Antoninus Pius appear on coins, so perhaps there is some explanation for this omission linked to the lack of popularity of Commodus who set up the column, rather than any lack of affection for his father Marcus. It may be that the novelty of the columnal form of monument had worn off and its depiction was no longer seen as significant or interesting, or it may simply be that, if the column was not completed till AD 192, Commodus might only have lived a few months or weeks after its dedication, not time enough for the column to be deemed a pertinent symbol to appear on the imperial coinage. Certainly Commodus's *damnatio memoriae* soon after his death would finally have scotched any such plans, had they indeed existed.

Contrasting perspectives

Given that the column is one of the best preserved ancient monuments in Rome, albeit quite heavily restored, it is not altogether surprising that it has been a focus for scholarly activity for centuries. While it would perhaps be too glib and easy to say that, 'every generation gets the column it deserves', in terms of each publication in some way overtly or covertly reflecting the political, cultural or intellectual obsessions of its day, this is to some extent true.[38] The opportunity will be taken here to discuss some of the major themes that have emerged through the study of the column over the years, though care will be taken not to become enmeshed in the threads of debate that have been spun around the column until some scholars have tied themselves in intellectual knots, placing almost as much emphasis on how the column has been studied as on the physical column itself. Perspectives centred on a gendered interpretation of the column will be discussed fully in Chapter Six.

The scholarly debate around the column has to some extent been fuelled by the existence of a full, high-quality black-and-white photographic record of the column frieze available to scholars since the late nineteenth century, when scaffolding was erected to facilitate this photographic recording project. Such a record favours the eye of the modern scholarly viewer over the ancient Roman viewer in that it provides equally clear, unrestricted viewing of every scene on the frieze, whether at the column's foot or towards its top. Every human figure on the frieze is equally viewable, every small gesture made can be seen and interpreted. Facial expressions of individual protagonists can even be made out. In other words, scholars have a fuller and more complete access to the column's visual narrative than any ancient viewer ever had, or indeed, was ever intended to have.

But this photographic record, published as a huge volume by Petersen, von Domaszewski and Calderini in 1896, has perhaps distorted the viewing of the column frieze in other ways. A photographic print by its very nature is a two-dimensional, square or rectangular image and by chopping up the Aurelian frieze, in reality a tactile, continuous unfurling frieze on a curved surface, into a series of individual photographic prints defining individual scenes, the nature of the frieze has been altered.[39] A comparison between plates 16 and 17 in this present volume will help to illustrate this point. However, there is no denying that the published photographic record is a remarkable and important resource for scholars of the column and of Roman art in general and that once the biases inherent in this record are acknowledged then the photographic prints, if used with care, can enhance our understanding of the monument. There are, of course, other illustrative records of the column which are helpful to use in tandem

15 Commodus as Hercules. Museo del Palazzo
dei Conservatori, Rome. (Photo: Author)

with Petersen's photographic record and mention has already been made of the
sixteenth-century drawings of the column base. In addition, there are numerous
subsequent drawn views of the column and some useful more detailed drawings
of parts of the frieze, including a volume of engravings with a commentary
Columna Antonina by P.S. Bartoli and G.P. Bellori, published in 1675.

It has already been noted that, while the Column of Marcus Aurelius owed
a great deal to its forerunner Trajan's Column, the way that the friezes have
been designed on Marcus's column must not simply be seen as a reaction to the
invisibility of many scenes on the earlier column, for these changes did not make
the later column more readable except for the lower frieze scenes and where
emphasis was placed on specific elements such as the figure of the emperor.
Both columns presented stories in the form of dislocated narrative vignettes
about specific wars, Trajan's Dacian wars on the earlier column and Marcus's
Marcomannic wars on the later one; these then were stories *about* the wars, not the
definitive stories *of* those wars. These were imagistic accounts, not documentary
histories, as some scholars have attempted to portray them.[40] This present book
has therefore eschewed the opportunity to provide a scene-by-scene description
of the column's frieze and then to try and relate the events depicted to events
described in the historical sources, with the notable exception of the depictions
on the column of the Weather Miracles. This is very much in keeping with present
scholarly opinion on how the column frieze should be studied.

Trajan's Column and the Column of Marcus Aurelius are compared at length elsewhere in this book, but care has been taken there to avoid the kind of scholarly comparison of the two monuments that has to a small degree blighted study of the Aurelian column, as some scholars have suggested that that the later column is not only a copy of the earlier column in its form, thus damning the later column as unoriginal in itself, but have also claimed that the later column is a less well-accomplished piece of work, thus damning it for a second time as being debased art, if not actually bad art. This judgemental positioning has even led to a marked difference in the way that the two columns have been studied or written about.

For some years the literature on Trajan's Column has contained reference to the existence of a *Maestro* – a Master – (a term first coined by the Italian art historian Ranuccio Bianchi Bandinelli) responsible for the design and execution of the column and its frieze and whose genius has been lauded by a number of subsequent authors in a manner that borders on the hero worship of this shadowy and, it must be remembered, altogether fictitious character.[41] The existence of no such *maestro* has been posited for the Aurelian column, perhaps because of the sometimes overt and sometimes less blatantly stated view that this column and its decorated frieze are poor, second-rate pieces of work in comparison to the Trajanic *Maestro's* masterpiece. Another academic strategy that differentiates study of one column from that of the other is the sometimes laboured use of cinematic vocabulary to describe the narrative programme of the Trajanic column,[42] a descriptive methodology that again has not been used for the Aurelian column, perhaps because, to overstretch the cinematic theme, Trajan's Column is seen as 'Powell and Pressburger' to the Aurelian Column's 'Hammer Horror'.

Another major theme of intellectual enquiry into the column's frieze has centred on the issue of what is known as 'frontality', that is the trend towards depicting human figures facing out towards the viewer, in other words viewing these figures frontally.[43] Frontality is seen as being one of the stylistic markers of the art of Late Antiquity and thence of early Medieval art, as opposed to being a relatively uncommon trait in the classical art of the earlier Roman Empire, leaving aside the issue of the character of the many hybrid provincial arts that flourished under the empire. Many scholars have claimed to find, or have chosen to see, numerous instances of the frontality of figures on the Aurelian column's frieze and have thus declared the monument to be representative of what German art historians have dubbed the *Stilwandel*,[44] the change of style that differentiates classical art from Late Antique art. In other words, the column has been seen by some authorities as being a transitional monument between the two art styles. Others, however, have questioned whether the column really is a transitional monument of this kind and, indeed, whether the many suggested instances of frontal depiction are of any great significance in this respect. It has even been suggested that some scholars have been too over-reliant in their use of photographs of scenes on the column's frieze, studying these two-dimensional, flat, cropped images in isolation and using them to identify frontality in scenes which, when viewed on the tactile, curving surface of the spiral frieze itself, appear less frontally biased than on the photographic prints. Indeed, this questioning of the 'reality' of the photographic record of this and other monuments has become quite a common theme in contemporary art historical writing on Roman art, almost to the point of obsession.[45]

Certainly the emperor appears on the column most usually in a frontal pose but this is most likely simply another of the strategies used to enhance the visibility of his images on the column, along with repetition, vertical ordering of his images, size differential between the emperor and other mortal figures, and, as is discussed elsewhere, the use of colour or gilding to pick him out. But other unusual strategies of representation are also used on the column frieze, suggesting that the artist/designer was trying out a number of stylistic strategies for clarity of viewing and that 'frontality' of some images was just one of many artistic tactics employed. Great use is made of individual turf lines for some figures to stand on, rather than the border at the bottom of the frieze forming the only ground surface for figures to walk or stand on, thus sometimes giving greater spatial depth to scenes by creating foreground, middle ground and background. Another tactic that is used occasionally is to employ an overhead, almost aerial, view of part of a scene, as seen in the portrayal of a river in one scene, and in another where boats appear to be viewed from above.

16 The Roman army crosses a pontoon bridge and soldiers deal with female barbarian prisoners. Scenes LXXXIV and LXXXV. The Column of Marcus Aurelius, Rome. (Photo DAIR 55.1066)

17 The Roman army crosses a pontoon bridge. Scene LXXXIV. The Column of Marcus Aurelius, Rome. (Photo: Graham Norrie, after Petersen *et al.* 1896)

There have even been instances of scholarly research on the column being influenced by nationalist agendas, in one case German and in another fascist Italian. When seeking financial sponsorship from German sources to enable him to compile and publish a comprehensive photographic record of the frieze on the column – a vastly expensive undertaking at the time and one that even today in the era of mechanical hoists, digital cameras and electronic publishing would be financially prohibitive for any individual scholar – Eugen Petersen stressed that his project had as one of its major objectives the study of the native Germanic peoples portrayed on the column. This was probably a winning gambit in terms of securing royal patronage for his project.[46] The Column of Marcus Aurelius was one of many monuments in Rome from which casts were taken to be displayed together in a major exhibition, the Augustan Exhibition of Roman Culture in 1937 and which are now in the Museo della Civiltà Romana in a suburb of Rome.[47] This major exhibition was staged by Mussolini as a way of validating his rule as successor to Augustus and the Roman emperors in the eyes of the world. One can only wonder what the effect may have been of the display of images of Romans slaughtering ethnic Germans on any Nazi dignitaries visiting the exhibition.

To Honour Famous Men

Throughout this book, although its principal subject is the Column of Marcus Aurelius, inevitably constant comparative reference is made to the earlier Trajan's Column, which all authorities agree to have been the conscious model for the later column both in terms of its form and function and its decoration. Questioning how the two columns differed, however, and why they differed in certain respects, is important for our understanding of the changing rhetoric of imperial art between the reigns of the two emperors or, more properly, between the reigns of Hadrian and Commodus. Hadrian oversaw the furbishment of Trajan's own column with a decorated frieze, while Commodus undertook the building, decorating and dedication of the column to Marcus.

In this chapter a brief introductory exposition on the use of free-standing columns in general in the classical and Roman world will therefore be followed by a discussion of Trajan's Column, in which this monument and its artworks will be set in their broader contemporary context. What the major monuments of Trajan's reign and their artworks together tell us about the relationship between Roman and barbarian at the time of Trajan and about the image of the emperor Trajan himself is highly significant in terms of setting the agenda for imperial art for many decades.

Early columns

While Marcus's column is perhaps, sometimes unfairly, dismissed as a copycat version of the earlier Trajan's Column, it is worth briefly considering here how columns in general were used as a building type in Rome and, indeed, how Trajan's Column itself was not in fact original in its form, though it certainly was almost entirely novel in terms of its decorative scheme.

While Trajan's Column was certainly the first column in Rome to be set up as an imperial monument with a decorated helical frieze around its shaft, it was not the first column to be erected here, nor was it the first imperial columnar monument.[1] Pliny in his *Natural History* tells us that, as early as the late fifth century BC, Republican Rome had adopted the Greek practice of erecting free-standing plain columns with statues on top. Pliny lists the pre-imperial precedents, a discussion which is confirmed by other sources, and tells us that these columns stood in various public places, for example, in forums and circuses. Such columns, both simple and more complex in design, were intended to honour individual citizen benefactors.

Precedents for decorating column shafts at least in part by relief carving come from ancient Egypt, from Greece (probably as a result of Egyptian influence) and, perhaps surprisingly, from Mainz in Roman *Germania*, where in the reign of Nero a Jupiter Column with a fully-decorated shaft was set up some time between AD 58 and AD 67. This column consisted of a shaft composed of five drums of diminishing size on which nineteen mythological figures were depicted. A gilded bronze statue of Jupiter stood on top of the column.

Pre-Trajanic imperial use of columnar monuments is attested both in Rome and elsewhere. Under Augustus four monumental columns were set up in Rome to honour Augustus and Agrippa after their victory in Egypt, perhaps under the influence of the form of Egyptian obelisks. Tiberius is said to have set up a granite column supporting his statue in the forum at Antioch, the column bearing the image of an eye. In the time of Claudius six monumental columns supporting statues of local dignitaries were set up in Sagalassus in Pisidia in the eastern empire. Only later did decorated columns become imperial forms of monument, with columns being erected in Rome to the emperors Trajan, Antoninus Pius (the latter with a plain but coloured shaft and a decorated base) and Marcus Aurelius and in Constantinople to the emperor Theodosius. Columns as an architectural form, therefore, became as firmly linked with the imperial order as arches had already become.

Trajan's Column, dating to AD 113, then, sets a number of precedents of its own. There have been some suggestions that an earlier column honouring Trajan, with decorated base and plain shaft, had initially been set up elsewhere in Rome and that it was subsequently taken down, re-erected, remodelled and provided with a carved frieze up the shaft under the aegis of Hadrian, in order to honour his late-adopted father Trajan. This theory, however, is though without much supporting evidence other than the appearance of an image of a plain-shafted column on some coin issues.[2] Trajan's Column as originally envisaged was probably not intended to be anything other than an honorific column, admittedly an honorific column of an altogether grander and more elaborate kind than had been seen in Rome before. However, the column was soon to take on a funerary role with the burial of the cremated remains of Trajan and Plotina in its base under the auspices of Hadrian. Just as there were precedents for columns being used for honorific commemoration, so too were there precedents for columns associated with Roman funerary commemoration. Lisa Vogel, in her study of the Column of Antoninus Pius,[3] cites literary evidence for this practice and discusses a number of such examples, including a tomb monument at Ostia that incorporates a column, a sepulchral column at Yaar near Baalbek in Syria, the tomb of Septumia at Pompeii, and, in an imperial context at Rome itself, 'there is evidence … for a column used for the cenotaph of Julius Caesar, and for one proposed as a cenotaph for Galba'.[4]

A chronologically intermediate column between that of Trajan and Marcus was the Column of Antoninus Pius set up by Marcus and Lucius Verus to honour their late adopted father in AD 161. The form of this monument was as highly original in its way as Trajan's Column had been at the time of its construction. Though the column shaft on the Column of Antoninus Pius was plain, it was made of red granite to contrast with the white marble decorated base, a striking and original touch.

The decorated base, which survives intact in the collections of the Vatican Museums in Rome, has individual scenes carved on panels on three of the four faces of the base.[5] The dedicatory inscription also survives on the fourth side. Opposite the side with the inscription is a classical scene of the apotheosis of Antoninus Pius and Faustina the Elder (*18*) that has evident stylistic links to the depiction of the apotheosis of Hadrian's empress Sabina on the *Arco di Portogallo*.[6] Yet, in almost complete contrast to this overtly classical scene in style, are the scenes on the other two decorated sides (*19*). These are of a *decursio* in both instances, which is a ritual military manoeuvre carried out as part of the rites at an imperial funeral, usually involving the anti-clockwise circling of the funeral pyre, although the pyre is not depicted here and the cavalrymen instead circle a detachment of foot soldiers. The almost identical scenes on the two faces are particularly worthy of note here because of their stylistic originality and their complete difference in style to the apotheosis scene. While in the latter scene the artist set large high-relief figures in an uncluttered composition against a plain background, in the *decursio* scenes, although high-relief carving against a plain background is again employed, the individual figures are very small indeed, almost like figures on a sarcophagus panel, rather than a panel on a major monument. Both the cavalry and infantry troops are positioned on individual groundlines, like pieces of turf, and the artist has played around with the perspective, with the central troops posed frontally and the circling cavalrymen posed as if seen from above. This monument will be discussed again in Chapter Six in relation to the portrayal of the empress Faustina the Elder on its base and of a similar cavalry scene to the *decursio* in Chapter Eight.

In opting to look not at the Column of Antoninus Pius as a model for the column dedicated to his father and mother but rather to go back further into Rome's archive of imperial monuments and to select Trajan's Column as his model, Commodus was perhaps making a number of statements about himself through this choice. Firstly, this choice allowed Commodus to stress his direct bloodline to Marcus and Faustina, rather than position himself as simply another adopted son of the Antonine dynasty. However, this dynastic link was, in fact, made by siting the column in a zone of monuments, which by virtue of their grouping, celebrated the dynasty itself rather than individual emperors *per se*.[7] Secondly, it allowed Commodus to position Marcus in direct succession to Trajan, the soldier emperor,

18 Apotheosis scene on the base of the Column of Antoninus Pius. Vatican Museums, Rome. (Photo: Author)

19 *Decursio* scene on the base of the Column of Antoninus Pius. Vatican Museums, Rome. (Photo: Author)

an image which Commodus was evidently keen to stress, despite his own recantation of his father's frontier policies and military campaigning. One lesson that was learned, however, from the Column of Antoninus Pius was that the decoration on base panels of such a monument could be used to get simple but powerful messages across in an accessible manner to the Roman viewer, for whom the proximity of the base made it a primary zone of visibility perfect for putting across political ideas.

Trajan's Column

Dedicated in AD 113, four years before Trajan's death, the column was completed under his successor Hadrian, probably with Apollodorus of Damascus as chief architect and designer.[8] Standing one hundred and twenty-eight Roman feet in height, the white Luna marble Trajan's Column would have dominated the new forum complex in which it was erected (*20*).[9] The column was intended to be an integral element in the forum's design. Indeed, even the dedicatory inscription on the basal plinth of the column refers to the quarrying and removal of vast quantities of rock and soil from the site before building works could commence, as if to stress the sheer effort put into urban regeneration during Trajan's reign, rather than it simply being an era of war and crisis as many at Rome feared it was at the time. The sheer grandiose scale of the forum and related contemporary works

20 General view of Trajan's Column, Rome. (Photo: Author)

was intended as a statement on the economic benefits of the emperor's costly and, in some quarters, heavily-criticised expansionist Dacian wars; subsequent generations, indeed, came to recognise Trajan's place as the best of emperors.

For those at Rome who had doubted the wisdom of Trajan's Dacian enterprise, such doubts would now have been alleviated not only by the military victories achieved, but also by the economic benefits to Rome that accrued from the spoils of those wars and which were used to finance the brash new building schemes in Rome. The most explicit link between conquest and commerce was made by the construction of the huge new market complex to the north of the forum, its very monumentality testifying to the grand scope of Trajan's vision for Rome. Trajan's Forum, inaugurated in AD 112, was the last and largest of the great forums here at the heart of the empire.

The column consisted of a massive decorated base on which were set nineteen column drums, with two further blocks forming the pedestal at the top on which would have originally stood a bronze statue of the emperor. The column shaft was decorated with an intricate carved, helical frieze two hundred metres long, carved in low relief and, either in whole or in part, painted and gilded, with small bronze accessories being attached to figures on the frieze in places (*21*). The column base contained a door that led to a chamber where the golden urn containing the emperor's ashes would probably have been housed and a stone spiral staircase leading up to the viewing platform at the top, the staircase being lit by a series of forty slit windows.

Three sides of the pedimental base of the column were carved with images of captured Dacian arms and armour, piled up as trophies, with some carvings of weapons also appearing on the fourth side, the front of the base, and perhaps representing an actual temporary victorious display of such material here before the dedication and building of the column. But it is the spiral relief sculptures around the column that are of particular interest to the present study. While it was probably not originally intended that the column shaft would be decorated, as can be ascertained from the fact that the windows are not integrated into the frieze design in the way that this been harmoniously achieved on the Column of Marcus Aurelius, nevertheless the addition of the decorated sculptural frieze was achieved relatively harmoniously and would have given the column an extra filip of originality in its use as a medium for conveying the intended imperial messages to its viewers. It has been suggested that the frieze was added after Trajan's death in AD 117 when the monument was allowed to become the emperor's tomb.

Around two thousand six hundred individual figures are represented in the frieze in around one hundred and fifty-five separate scenes. The reliefs allude to Trajan's two Dacian wars of AD 101–106. Various scholars have attempted to match events on the column reliefs to historical accounts of the emperor's campaigns, but the reliefs cannot truly be called historical documents, nor can they be interpreted strictly as war reportage, as they have sometimes been viewed.[10] However, they do provide the most detailed statement on the nature of Roman imperial power at the peak of the empire's expansion. Artistic influences on the design of the frieze

21 Part of the decorated frieze on Trajan's Column, Rome. (Photo: Author)

on Trajan's Column must have included traditional Roman triumphal paintings, earlier imperial reliefs such as the processional scenes on the *Ara Pacis* or Augustan Altar of Peace or on the Arch of Titus, and possibly also illustrated scrolls.

As on the Column of Marcus Aurelius, the scenes on the frieze on Trajan's Column can be divided up into a number of basic themes: scenes involving the emperor and stressing his central role in the events portrayed; scenes involving events that may be rooted in historical reality; scenes involving Roman deities aiding or abetting the Roman forces or celebrating their victories; scenes involving the Roman army undertaking non-violent tasks such as marching or building camps and fortifications; scenes involving the Roman army in battle; scenes involving barbarian defeat and submission, including mass suicides and the corralling of prisoners for shipping to Rome as slaves; and scenes involving non-Roman women, both Romanised women and barbarian women, most of these scenes also being categorised under the other main thematic headings listed here. Some of the column scenes categorised in this thematic schema will now be individually discussed. The numbering system used to locate individual scenes is that devised by Cichorius and followed by most subsequent researchers.

Trajan appears on the column frieze fifty-nine times, often at the centre of dense multi-figure compositions (*22*).[11] As might be expected, he is depicted numerous times sacrificing, addressing the army, taking military counsel, receiving delegations and receiving prisoners for condemnation or clemency. He travels with the army and, in fact, his positioning in many scenes suggests to the viewer that he is one of the army, the consummate soldier-emperor. From certain viewpoints the placing of the image of the emperor would seem to invite the viewer to link certain images in sequence vertically rather than attempt to read the frieze horizontally as a matter of course. Richard Brilliant has highlighted one such vertical juxtaposition between Trajan addressing the troops – an *adlocutio* – in Scene x, Trajan again in Scene xix portrayed almost frontally, and the figure of Victory in Scene lxxviii.

Of the scenes involving the emperor and stressing his central role in the events portrayed, one scene in particular (Scene xxxvi) would appear to be significant in its contrasting of Roman civilisation and non-Roman primitive barbarity, a contrastive theme explored in a number of ways on the column using different visual counterpoints and where a scene of non-violent action was subtly used to make as highly-charged a political point as battle scenes do elsewhere on the column. In this scene, Trajan, evidently on his way to the war, is depicted with his entourage and general staff, entering a provincial town, probably in Moesia. He is greeted there by the enthusiastic local population, men, women and children, in a scene of inclusivity, with not solely male officials being represented, as was so often the case. To paraphrase Natalie Boymel Kampen who first made this observation, the presence of women and children in this scene stresses the importance of a civilised and protective environment for this community, for these families, provided under the rule of Rome. It suggests a guarantee of future

22 Trajan with the army in Scene XLII. Trajan's Column, Rome. (Photo: copyright F.A. Lepper and S.S. Frere)

prosperity in both the public and private spheres.[12] The lives of these people had been transformed under Roman patronage and imperialism. Once barbarians themselves, according to the Roman definition, these barbarians have been transformed into citizens or proto-citizens from a legal point of view, if not necessarily into equals in the minds of those at Rome. The positive relationship between these people and Rome contrasts significantly with the scenes unfolding above in which war becomes the only point of cultural contact and exchange between the Dacian peoples and Rome.

In another scene involving Trajan, which perhaps can only have been intended as a joke of some sort (Scene IX), a barbarian man, perhaps an emissary of some kind it has been suggested, although he could simply be a local man, is depicted in the act of falling off a mule as he passes by the emperor and two attendant officers standing on higher ground behind him. Has he been overawed by the presence of the great emperor?

On the column demonstrable scenes involving events that may be rooted in historical reality are in effect few, though some academics nevertheless have attempted at length to see historicity in all of the scenes on the column frieze from beginning to end. As has already been noted, attempts to read the column frieze from beginning to end, from bottom to top like this in order to interpret the succession of events as representing a narrative history of the Dacian wars, are doomed to failure. While Richard Brilliant has noted that, 'there is a historical program, arranged not just successively by scenes but in collections or groups of scenes that incorporate larger chronological units or periods in episodic form', he goes on to note that 'since the fundamental connection among events is casual, fixed in Trajan, precise location in time and space becomes less important'.[13] Certainly attested by the historical sources and depicted on other works of art including the Great Trajanic Frieze, the *Tropaeum Traiani* at Adamklissi and the tombstone of Tiberius Claudius Maximus from Philippi, is the suicide of the Dacian leader Decebalus, following the successful storming of his mountaintop stronghold of Sarmizegethusa by the Roman forces and their pursuit of the fugitive king (Scene CXLV).[14] On the column the moment of Decebalus's death is caught *in stasis*, literally seconds before the arrival on horseback of the Roman officer Tiberius Claudius Maximus, who was subsequently to behead the body of the Dacian chieftain and cut off his right hand as trophies to present to the emperor (*23*). The actual scene of the mutilation of Decebalus's corpse was not depicted on the column.

While Decebalus's suicide could be seen as a brave act, a final flourish of defiance which would rob the Roman victors of his participation in a stage-managed triumph in Rome, it can also be viewed as an act of self-authorship; an attempt to regain in death some form of control over his own destiny, if no longer over that of his people. But Maximus' act of beheading turned the act of self-authorship

23 The death of Decebalus. Scene CXLV. Trajan's Column, Rome. (Photo: copyright F.A. Lepper and S.S. Frere)

around on itself in a most macabre fashion, with the Dacian leader's severed head being depicted as a trophy in other scenes on the Column. Such a portrayal of victory over even death itself may have been used to provide further testament to the superiority of the Roman forces and of Roman imperial power. The symbol of the severed barbarian head is a powerful one that appears on both Trajan's Column and the Column of Marcus Aurelius, as will be discussed further below and in Chapter Eight.

One of the most extraordinary scenes (Scene XLV) on Trajan's Column is set in a fortress or town, where a number of Dacian women are depicted torturing Roman prisoners. Alternatively, it has been suggested that the women, rather than being Dacian, are in fact Moesian women taking revenge on these men, who are themselves Dacian and not Roman, for their incursion into the Moesian province and the slaughter of their husbands or sons who were loyal to Rome.[15] The camp in which the torture takes place is therefore interpreted as a Roman fort, though there is nothing to confirm this interpretation on the column scene. This alternative reading, therefore, is unproven and seems unlikely. The torture scene was positioned relatively low down on the column's shaft – being part of the seventh spiral up from the start of the base – perhaps suggesting that it conveyed a particular message that was important to convey to all viewers. Even if they could not easily see other incidents elsewhere on the column, this particular scene would be clearly discernible even from the ground.

In the upper part of the scene, two Roman captives have been stripped naked and appear to be bound with their hands tied behind their backs. Two barbarian women stand to either side of the prisoners, each somehow striking or prodding at the helpless men, each of whom has his head turned away from the women, perhaps in pain. Beneath the walls, in the lower part of the scene, a third, bound Roman captive sprawls on a rocky outcrop, while a Dacian woman stands over him and appears to be jabbing him with a stake as he recoils in evident agony.

The very unusual nature of this scene – it is unique in Roman art – suggests that it could be a representation of an actual event from the wars, though one that has not survived in any historical account and which has not been represented on any other Trajanic monument. On the other hand, it could be a fictional scene, one created by the artist to make a particular point about the cruelty inherent in the Dacian people, even among the women, and in some way to partly justify the wars. The torture scene may have been intended both as an indicator of barbarian cruelty in general and of the 'otherness' of barbarian women in particular.

Scenes involving Roman deities aiding or abetting the Roman forces or celebrating their victories include the depiction of a benign river god overseeing the Roman forces crossing a bridge over the Danube in Scene III, a giant figure of Victory inscribing details of Trajan's triumphs on a large shield in Scene LXXVIII, a male deity, *Jupiter Tonans*, aiding the Roman forces in battle in Scene XXIV by hurling a thunderbolt at the enemy troops and a female personification of night, probably Nyx, helping to provide cover for the Roman forces in battle (Scene XXXVIII).

Scenes involving the Roman army undertaking non-violent tasks such as being on the march or building camps and fortifications are numerous and repetitive.[16] The range of non-violent subjects is wide and even includes a scene of soldiers foraging for plants (Scene CX). Many previous studies of the column have used the scenes on the shaft as a rich source of material for understanding the operation of the Roman army in the field at this time, the images often being read in tandem with historical accounts of the Roman army at war.[17] Certainly these scenes provide much detailed visual information about military equipment, about arms and armour and, indeed, about the building of camps and bridges and about military manoeuvres. However, such a line of enquiry is eschewed here in favour of a political reading of the column's decorative programme. As a general observation, on the column the figures of the Dacians are often used in a purely contrastive way, dismantling their fortresses before the arrival of Roman forces, in contrast to an almost exaggerated concentration on the building and construction work being carried out by the Roman troops. Perhaps significantly, these troops are almost exclusively legionaries rather than auxiliaries. This seems to be part of an overall narrative thread that stresses a sense of overwhelming order amongst the victors and disorder among the defeated barbarians, a distinction that was to be emphasised in a much less subtle way on the later Column of Marcus Aurelius.

On Trajan's Column the Dacians are also quite commonly depicted in forests and woods, or up in the mountains, as opposed to being shown in their towns or their fortresses, thus possibly creating in the viewer's mind a visual opposition between nature, as represented by the Dacians, and culture, as represented by the Romans, and thus between barbarity and civilisation respectively. This is quite possibly another example of a nostalgia trend, a longing for a purer and simpler state of being, that had previously occurred in Hellenistic Greek and some Roman portrayals of Celts or Gauls. The Romans, therefore, are being portrayed to the viewers as masters of the physical environment and nature itself, as well as being masters of the physical bodies and minds of conquered peoples.

Scenes involving the Roman army in battle are not as numerous as an initial viewing might indicate. Indeed, they take up perhaps only a quarter of the column's surface area. Certainly there are far fewer battle scenes on the column than there are on the Column of Marcus Aurelius and they do not dwell upon the bloody realities of war, as is very much the case on the later column. However, the artists did not flinch from including one or two jarring scenes that do not sit well with modern sensibilities but which would not perhaps have been seen as being out of place by the ancient Roman viewer. It is true to say that, in comparison with some later monuments, including Marcus's column, the portrayal of war on Trajan's Column is perhaps surprisingly sanitised. It has been suggested that the relatively few, and usually formulaic, battle scenes reflected the deliberate desire in the conception of the monument to address a fear of the army – its soldiers, its independence and its power – among the population of Rome, by playing down this aspect of the column. That is, it was a monument to Trajan the soldier-emperor and to his glorious victories in the Dacian wars but not to the Roman army itself.

On Trajan's Column some particularly bloodthirsty acts by the Roman forces were portrayed openly. For instance, the beheading of the dead Decebalus towards the end of the second war, discussed above, was not the only instance of this practice depicted on the column. In Scene XXIV, in the midst of a hectic skirmish between Roman and Dacian infantry forces outside a wood, stands a Roman trooper with his short sword in one hand and a shield in the other. He prepares to fight off a Dacian opponent who raises his own sword to strike a blow at the Roman. The Roman soldier has already taken a battlefield trophy, a Dacian head, and this he grips in his teeth, by the hair, in order to keep his hands free for battle. The head hangs down in front of him, blood dripping, this blood perhaps being originally rendered in paint when the Column was inaugurated. In Scene LVI, outside a Roman encampment, two bearded Dacian heads are displayed mounted on posts and in Scene LXXII two heads are offered as trophies to the emperor himself by Roman troopers.[18]

Scenes involving barbarian defeat and submission, including mass suicides and the corralling of prisoners for shipping to Rome as slaves, appear a number of times and help to emphasise, rather than overemphasise, the scale of the Roman victories in the wars. Elsewhere on the Column (Scene CXL, for instance) the suicides of other Dacian leaders are depicted. This narrative of the death of the power and lineage of the Dacian male aristocracy, together with the forced transportation of female Dacian noblewomen into exile, tells a powerful story of the ending of Dacian élite lineage in its present form and of an uncertain future for the surviving women of this élite, relocated in the political, social and sexual framework of Roman society.

Finally, scenes involving non-Roman women, both Romanised women and barbarian women, are notable for their presence, their number and the subtlety of their use in the overall narrative here of Roman imperial power.[19] A number of such scenes have already been discussed under the other main thematic groupings identified on the column. As has been noted by a number of authorities, the women depicted here are shown as being mothers accompanied by children, they usually appear in female groups and usually in the company of men. Their dress and appearance is generally modest and organised. Their presence is a deliberate strategy to help emphasise certain of the messages given out by the column frieze to its viewers. While women and children are depicted being captured on the column in a number of scenes and fleeing the Roman advance into barbarian territory elsewhere, they are not depicted as being at the centre of violent action as they often are on the Column of Marcus Aurelius, as is discussed in detail in Chapter Six. Images of women's bodies suffering are not employed on Trajan's Column as metaphors for the Roman conquest and dominion over barbarian lands and peoples as they are on Marcus's column.

Viewing

While the Column of Marcus Aurelius in Rome might be dismissed by some as a debased copy of Trajan's Column in both form and content, a close analysis of the artwork on the later column shows that the two monuments could not be more different in terms of the political and social ideologies represented. While the problems inherent in viewing the middle and upper portions of the frieze on Trajan's Column would have been alleviated by the original appearance of the sculptures as painted and enhanced with the addition of metal or even wooden fixtures and those with access to the libraries on either side of the column would have had an easier and more privileged viewing, nevertheless much of the dense and detailed frieze would not have been visible at all. Such concerns, however, do not seem to have troubled the sculptors, either in designing the column friezes in the first place or in the manner of the execution of the sculptures themselves; those at the top of the column are as detailed and well-executed as those at the bottom. On the Column of Marcus Aurelius the size of the individual figures was increased, less background was created and there were fewer spirals of the frieze, all doubtless deliberate strategies to make the artwork more readable, even if still virtually impossible to follow in sequence around the shaft of the column.

Nevertheless, it would have been impossible for any Roman viewer to 'read' Marcus's column in the manner that can be achieved today by reference to the full photographic surveys of the monument undertaken when the provision of scaffolding for repair work and conservation was available, for instance, and to casts of the reliefs taken on a number of occasions, including those prepared for the great Fascist-sponsored Augustan Exhibition of Roman Culture of 1937 and now on display in Rome at the Museo della Civiltà Romana.

It must be assumed that Trajan's Column was intended to make a direct appeal to the eye of the viewer through its daringly original form and dense decorative scheme. If the viewer were then to take away an impression of the artworks as a suitable commemoration of the victories and achievements of the emperor Trajan, then it would have served its fundamental purpose. To achieve this, the scenes in which the emperor himself appeared were very clearly-positioned, almost in a vertical plane, to stress his centrality to the unfolding drama of the campaigns in Dacia. Closer inspection would have provided additional insights into the artistic programme and repeated viewings would have allowed for further revelations and detail to emerge through the reading of individual scenes. The sheer density of the artwork and the great number of scenes presented, with hundreds of human figures playing out the incessant drama, allowed for as many readings to be made as there would have been, and continue to be, viewers of the column.

Manipulating history

It is from Trajan's reign that perhaps the largest body of Roman portrayals of barbarians has survived, not only on the column, but on a number of other major monuments in Rome and elsewhere. While to some extent this is a reflection of an element of chance in historical survival, on the other hand it perhaps also reflects the sheer importance of contact with the barbarian world in the political and ideological make-up of his reign.

Through an examination of the four key surviving monuments associated with the reign of Trajan – Trajan's Column and the Great Trajanic Frieze in Rome, the Arch of Trajan at Benevento in southern Italy, and the so-called Trophy of Trajan at Adamklissi in present-day Romania – certain common themes can be seen to emerge in the way that seemingly simple and easily-understood images of barbarians were used to convey quite complex messages within the overall schema of each monument and of the reign as a whole, as discussed in detail in my previous book *Enemies of Rome. Barbarians Through Roman Eyes.*[20]

It is interesting to note that the Great Trajanic Frieze and the column, although ostensibly at first glance utilising the same repertoire of subject and imagery, were in reality very different in the way in which they presented the subject and deployed imagery to different ideological ends. In the whole of Roman imperial art there is no better illustration of the subtlety and nuance sometimes inherent in the use of images of barbarians in imperial art and rhetoric and of the way in which the historical veracity of an event could itself be inverted or bent out of shape through the manipulation of both time and the involvement of individual protagonists. In other words, the unreliable artistic narrator could misdirect the viewer in his or her reading of a particular scene or event and did so at this time. Even Trajan's portraits to some extent lied to the viewer about his age in the later part of his reign, to the extent that art historians today often refer to him as 'the ageless adult'.[21]

While Trajan's Column was not strictly historical commentary, nevertheless it was quasi-documentary in content. The Great Trajanic Frieze, on the other hand, was in a tradition of heroicising art, more commonly associated in the Hellenistic tradition with mythological representation in the form of battles between Greeks and Amazons, or involving Giants, Centaurs, or Lapiths. The emperor Trajan as depicted on the column was one with his army; he addressed his troops, he was on campaign with them, he observed their labours and battled against the Dacians, and so on. Indeed, the column frieze perhaps somewhat over-emphasised his direct involvement in the campaigning, for he was in all likelihood well behind the lines for much of the time. However, on part of the Great Trajanic Frieze this direct imperial involvement is taken to even greater extremes of stretching credibility, with the mounted figure of Trajan being depicted in the very thick of frenzied battle. Once more, on one of the decorated metopes from the *Tropaeum Traiani* at Adamklissi, Trajan rides down a Dacian foe, perhaps even intended to be interpreted by the viewer as being Decebalus himself, the figure of the emperor having himself taken on the role of his famous officer Tiberius Claudius Maximus.

During Trajan's reign contact with barbarian peoples was principally undertaken through the policy of imperial expansion, pursued by war. In particular, the emperor's wars against the Dacians came to dominate the state art of Rome at this time and during the reign of his successor, the emperor Hadrian, who pursued the completion of some monuments started or conceived under Trajan. Indeed, it is probably true to say that the Dacian prisoner became the defining image of the age. Such images of foreign bodies as can be found on Trajan's Column and other major monuments of his reign acted as maps that helped position the viewer in geographical and cultural terms at the ideological centre of the empire.

3

The Fifth Good Emperor

Marcus Aurelius was viewed by the Romans as being their fifth good emperor after Nerva, Trajan, Hadrian and Antoninus Pius. It was therefore entirely in keeping with the further promoting of his place in this illustrious company, that Commodus chose to have Marcus depicted on his funerary, commemorative column as a soldier-emperor in the mould of Trajan, and, indeed, to have the column frieze designed in such a way as to lead the viewer's reading of the column through the privileging of Marcus's image there. An examination will now be made of the way in which this programme of casting Marcus as soldier-emperor was carried through, how Marcus was depicted on the column frieze and how, if at all, these posthumous images differed from images of the emperor created during his own lifetime and probably under his own auspices.

Transmission

The overall artistic programme of the Column of Marcus Aurelius has been examined by the art historian Richard Brilliant as part of a broader analysis of narrative styles in ancient art in his book *Visual Narratives: Storytelling in Etruscan and Roman Art* and there he concluded that Marcus's image had been positioned at various places on the column frieze in a deliberate, programmatic way, with these scenes featuring the emperor being further enhanced by various design strategies such as colouring or gilding.[1] A short summary of his main conclusions will be presented here.

Brilliant's analysis showed that Marcus appeared on his column sixty-two times and Trajan fifty-nine times on his earlier column, figures that are perhaps surprisingly close. However, Brilliant found that images of Marcus appeared thirty-six times on the lower half of his column, that is up to the depiction of Victory marking the end of the first war, where he would be more visible to viewers, and only twenty-six times thereafter.[2] Again, he concluded that Marcus's column:

> has many more ceremonial scenes and many fewer connectives, lessening the value
> of the tableau composition but strengthening the development of strong vertical
> accents, as the viewer's eye moves upward from one imperial ceremony to the
> next. Scenes of battle, the taking of captives, and acts of clemency … appear more

frequently on the bottom part of the Aurelian Column, where the emperor can more readily dominate the composition. For the same reason, the more purely ceremonial scenes, such as advent, address, and the departure for war are more common at the higher levels, where the simple organization of the hierarchical composition made the emperor stand out.[3]

The start of the unfurling of the decorated frieze, the first appearance of Marcus Aurelius and the figure of Victory all occur on the northeast side, facing the *Via Flaminia*. When viewed and linked vertically, the individual scenes involving the emperor in ceremonial situations lead the viewer's eye inexorably up the column face to finally alight on the statue of the emperor on top (or on statues of Marcus and Faustina if she too was represented by a statue). As Brilliant has pointed out, this verticality 'effectively disconnected the Imperial imagery from the helical course of putative history'.[4] Repetition enhanced the vertical effect.

Thus it would seem that the programmatic design of the column reliefs, following the lead of the design of Trajan's Column where such ideas were first formulated, allowed for three main types of viewing based on what Brilliant has called 'three distinct, but interrelated codes of varying degrees of narrativity: the *annalistic*, the *iconic*, and the *imagistic*'.[5] The first, annalistic, code allowed the viewer to understand from their encounter with the total monument, if we can call it this, that the monument alluded to victory in a war, an understanding that would have been enhanced by further viewing or subsequent viewings, particularly by taking in some of the details of the frieze and the decorated panels on the base. The second, iconic, code allowed the viewer to identify the emperor easily, as has been discussed in detail above, and to understand his *virtus* or virtuousness and also to understand his role in the victory in the war. The third, imagistic, mode allowed the viewer to gain an imagistic, non-linear impression of events in the war by viewing individual scenes in no set order in particular and to understand that these scenes related to events that contributed towards victory in the war without losing sight of the emperor's central role. What this really means is that there were intended to be as many different types of viewings of the column friezes as there would be viewers.

As Brilliant has also written, 'the whole form of the Column and its reliefs could be grasped at once as manifestation rather than as presentation. Casuality, sequence and demonstration, all related to the establishment of satisfactory connections between events, are denigrated by the new emphasis on the revelation of the Imperial *virtus* and on providence'.[6] To the viewer the programmatic organisation of scenes on the column rather than their sequential cohesion made possible 'the simultaneous apprehension of past, present and future events as revealed in the sculpted record'.[7]

A different kind of programmatic analysis of the column has been undertaken by Felix Pirson[8] who concentrated his analytical attention on the battle scenes that so dominate the column frieze and Pirson's analysis will be discussed more fully in Chapter Seven. The most recent theoretical approach to the study of the column frieze has been to distinguish between what is termed a 'horizontal reading' of the frieze and of individual scenes in the frieze where primacy is given to the narrative aspects of the artworks and a 'vertical reading' where primacy is given to an ideological reading of the scene or scenes.[9] Under this schema the process of horizontal reading is generally seen as old fashioned. The process of vertical reading on the other hand is seen as new and vital, though it has perhaps already become too enmeshed in the reading of gesture as the primary indicator of ideology.

The emperor and religious practice

In Chapter Four discussion will be concentrated on the two instances of divine intervention depicted on the column in the form of the Weather Miracles, a discussion which will touch upon the relationship between the emperor and the pagan gods of Rome. This relationship will be explored further here through looking at just one of the many appearances of Marcus on the column frieze officiating at religious ceremonies and fulfilling other religious duties. His role in overseeing the Roman army on campaign in the field will be discussed elsewhere.

The overall study of rites of the state religion as represented in Roman art in general was the subject of a major study by Inez Scott Ryberg carried out almost fifty years ago.[10] Although Roman art history has moved on considerably from the kind of study prepared by Ryberg, her work has generally stood the test of time and her views on the images of Marcus Aurelius carrying out his religious duties on the column are well worth summarising here. Each emperor's participation in the numerous and regular processions and sacrifices associated with the operation of the state religion provided them with a process by which they could regularly reassert their relationship with the Roman people.

The *suovetaurilia* was a triple sacrifice of animals, a bull, a sheep and a pig, which had become firmly associated with the person of the emperor in Roman state religion. Two instances of this rite occur on the column, both at the beginning of a season of campaigning, obviously in attempt to gain from the gods the most propitious circumstances for fighting the war by cleansing the Roman camp. The first scene is badly damaged and will not be discussed in detail here, the second scene (Scene xxx) being altogether more significant in that the correct procedures of the rite are not being carried out here, or perhaps more likely the artist has somehow failed to grasp the importance of these procedures when devising the scene (*24*). Again, as Ryberg has pointed out, an equally lackadaisical attitude to the significance and importance of religious rites is perhaps shown on the column by the almost perfunctory nature of other sacrificial scenes here.[11]

Given the significance of ritual practice and the importance seemingly attached

24 Marcus officiates at a sacrifice. Scene xxx. The Column of Marcus Aurelius, Rome. (Photo: Graham Norrie, after Petersen *et al.* 1896)

to his adherence to his duties to the gods by Marcus, it is perhaps surprising that this incorrect procedural passage of events should have been portrayed on a major public monument, albeit in a position on the column where detailed observation of the scene is not really possible for the viewer on the ground. Perhaps seeing that Marcus was present at the rite, and his figure was everywhere emphasised on the column whenever it appeared in order to aid the viewer, was sufficient for the purposes of the column's message. Again, the scene was perhaps more important here as an indicator of the opening of a military campaign than as a religious rite in itself.

The foreground of the scene is taken up with soldiers moving in line, perhaps in procession as part of the ceremony, the leading figure holding a staff or rod, the second in line, who wears a lion-skin on his head, carries a trumpet. The main focus of religious activity is in the upper register of the scene. Anyway, of the three expected sacrificial animals only the bull and sheep are present, although it could be that the artist had intended the viewer to assume that the third beast was present but out of sight. However, the fact that the animals are in the incorrect order of procession, reversed in fact, suggests the omission of the pig was a genuine error made in ignorance. To compound matters the official called the *popa* who normally accompanies the bull is here depicted leading the sheep and the expected flute player, whose task was to provide noise to keep away evil spirits, is not present, being replaced by a trumpeter playing his instrument at an odd angle more akin to the playing of a flute. This group is moving towards Marcus who stands at the right of the scene, near a small tripod, holding a *patera* and what is probably a scroll in his hands and with his robe drawn up over his head, as is usual for the officiating priest at such an occasion.

It has also been noted that in the many images of Marcus that appear on the column he is nearly always depicted turned to the right, seen as the favourable direction in Roman superstition, his right arm perpendicular to his body.[12] Not only would this have been seen by the Roman viewer as an extra-favourable trait in the emperor's favour but it would also have helped the spectator further in his or her attempt to locate the position of the figure of the emperor on the column shaft.

The column and the image of Marcus

Though the column was erected by Marcus's son Commodus and probably was not completed until about ten years after Marcus's death, it must nevertheless be examined from the point of view of how it presents the image of Marcus to the Roman people. In order to further explore this question it will be necessary briefly to review other artworks in Rome on which Marcus appears in order to see if these images provide any sort of continuum, or if Marcus on the column differs in some way from Marcus on these other monuments. As has been pointed out by one authority, Marcus's role on the column 'dominates the person of the emperor'.[13]

The appearances of Marcus on the column are numerous and he appears in a number of roles: sacrificing to the gods, addressing the troops, parlaying with the enemy and so on. Despite the fact that Marcus spent so much time absent from Rome, campaigning with the frontier army, nevertheless here he is, enshrined in stone for all to see, at the empire's heart, busy with the affairs of state. He is cast here as a soldier-emperor, like Trajan before him, in most of the images of him on the column, represented wearing military garb and taking a hands-on role in the minutiae of the campaigns. This image of Marcus the soldier-emperor would seem to be very much at odds with Marcus the philosopher-emperor, the author of the *Meditations*. Again, perhaps the very form of his column was meant to bring to its viewers' minds the connection with Trajan's Column and thus position Marcus alongside Rome's perhaps most renowned soldier-emperor who had overseen the expansion of the empire to its greatest extent under his reign.

One author has suggested that viewers of the two columns in the second century might not have distinguished between the images of warfare portrayed on Trajan's Column and those on the Column of Marcus Aurelius, that is between a war of conquest and expansion and a war of defence and attrition,[14] although this is not a point with which the present author concurs.

If Commodus planned to cast his late father in the role of a soldier-emperor and thus link him with Trajan, so it is possible that Commodus also had himself somehow cast in this drama, particularly as he, too, had played some role in his father's military campaigning and had thus legitimately celebrated a joint triumph with Marcus in AD 177, even though he had chosen not to pursue the military policies of his father following Marcus's death. As has been noted above, while there are no convincing identifications of a representation of Commodus on the column's frieze, it has been suggested that he may have appeared on the now-lost decorated column base. In the words of Penelope Davies, 'if he did stand at his father's side in the base frieze, Commodus's position as heir would have been explicit, and his

25 Marcus and his forces cross the Danube bridge. Scene III. The Column of Marcus Aurelius, Rome. (Photo: Graham Norrie, after Petersen *et al.* 1896)

26 Marcus
addresses the
troops. Scene IX.
The Column of
Marcus Aurelius,
Rome. (Photo:
Graham Norrie,
after Petersen *et al.*
1896)

legitimation implied through the dynastic heritage expressed in the column's topographical ties'.[15] Commodus's name would certainly have appeared on the original dedicatory inscription on the column base and it is also suggested that he appeared alongside Marcus in a scene of the celebration of a triumph on one of the decorated panel reliefs from a victory arch which probably stood nearby.

Marcus appears so many times on the column, often in stock scenes, that only a few of his appearances on the column are illustrated here, including his first appearance wearing a cuirass and, in the company of his general staff, accompanying his soldiers across the Danube bridge (Scene III) (*25*). On the other side of the river, in the second scene reproduced here, Marcus is now dressed in a *paludamentum* or military cloak to address the troops, flanked by officers and *signifers* (Scene IX) (*26*). Later on, higher up the column (Scene LXVI), the emperor is presented with the severed head of a male barbarian, a scene which is discussed more fully and illustrated in Chapter Eight. In three other scenes reproduced here the emperor can be seen: making an offering to the gods on a flaming altar, surrounded by a retinue of bearded staff officers and troops, all of whom closely resemble Marcus in appearance (Scene LXXV) (*27*); consulting with two officers outside a fortified Roman encampment inside which tented structures can be seen (Scene LXXX) (*28*); and positioned on a dais outside a large Romanised building either receiving barbarian emissaries, wearing conical hats on their heads, or offering these men clemency if they are, in fact, captured combatants (Scene XLIX) (*29*). In most of these scenes, probably again as part of the strategy to make the figure of the emperor more visible in each of his appearances on the column, Marcus is generally consciously isolated, apart from his usual small, close retinue of generals and advisers, so that he does not become lost in crowds of figures as Trajan often does on his column.

Marcus is also quite easily identifiable in the many scenes in which he appears because of the consistently carried out, portrait-like representation of the emperor with his neatly-coiffed hair and well-trimmed beard. Marcus's portrait busts that have come down to us move through four main types of image, from the youthful Marcus, the promising young man adopted into the imperial family, to the mature,

27 Marcus pours a libation on an altar. Scene LXXV. The Column of Marcus Aurelius, Rome. (Photo: Graham Norrie, after Petersen *et al.* 1896)

28 Marcus and officers outside a Roman camp. Scene LXXX. The Column of Marcus Aurelius, Rome. (Photo: Graham Norrie, after Petersen *et al.* 1896)

29 Marcus receives barbarian prisoners or emissaries. Scene XLIX. The Column of Marcus Aurelius, Rome. (Photo: Graham Norrie, after Petersen *et al.* 1896)

bearded emperor as also seen on the column. Diana Kleiner has described the emperor's portraits as showing him 'develop from a carefree and handsome crown prince to a militarily strong but merciful world ruler, and ultimately to a tired and disillusioned Stoic philosopher'.[16]

Marcus's mature portraits firmly place him in the tradition of Antonine representations established by his adopted father and predecessor, Antoninus Pius. The fourth and final portrait type which dates to between AD 170–180, known somewhat awkwardly to art historians as the 'Capitoline *Imperatori* 38' type, shows him with the same full head of carefully-curled hair that he possessed in his youth and middle years, but with a fuller beard, divided down the centre and arranged in individual parallel locks (*30*). Diana Kleiner sees portraits of this late type as 'extraordinary human documents because they not only incorporate the aging process but also mirror the state of mind of the philosopher-emperor. It is not surprising that the earliest instance of psychological penetration in Roman portraiture should coincide with the principate of a deep thinker thoroughly imbued with Stoic ideas'.[17]

While Commodus might have wanted the Roman public to equate Marcus on the column with the earlier emperor Trajan, it is interesting that during Marcus's own lifetime he was evidently happy to allow his official portraits, both in stone and on his coinage, to mirror his own aging in a way that Trajan himself had not. The 'ageless adult' emperor had wanted to hold back time with his portraits, while Marcus was happy to meet the onrush of time head on.

In August 2008, while this book was being completed, media reports were released of an extraordinary new discovery of fragments of a giant statue of Marcus at Sagalassus, in present-day southern Turkey. While excavations at the site will take some years to complete and publication of the findings of the work will be even later, some brief interim discussion of the statue found at Sagalassus will be presented here, based on the press coverage.[18]

The new discovery is of three fragments of a marble statue of Marcus, comprising the head, clearly a recognisible portrait head of the emperor, the right arm and parts of the lower legs and feet. It has been estimated that the original statue was about fifteen feet tall. It is, without a doubt, the best marble statue of the emperor that has yet been found, even in Rome and, along with the bronze equestrian statue of Marcus, it will doubtless come to define Marcus's image. It was found amongst a deposit of rubble inside the large *frigidarium* of the public baths, a room which has been identified as being dedicated to the rulers of the Antonine dynasty. Fragments of huge statues of Hadrian and possibly of his wife Sabina, and possibly of Antoninus Pius and his wife Faustina the Elder have also been found there. It is hoped that excavation will uncover further fragments of these statues and of a statue of Marcus's wife Faustina the Younger, which might be expected to have been set up there as well.

The head of Marcus, just under three feet in height, is very much the portrait of the philosopher-emperor. He holds in his right hand a small globe or orb to

30 Portrait bust of Marcus Aurelius. Museo Capitolino, Rome. (Photo DAIR 68.3822)

symbolise his earthly and divine power. The statue's legs are broken just above the knees but it is interesting to note that his feet are shod in army boots, decorated with a lion skin, tendrils and Amazon's shields.

Other significant images of Marcus appear on the so-called panel reliefs of Marcus Aurelius, derived from a monument, probably a victory arch or arches of some kind, erected between AD 176 and AD 180, to celebrate the emperor's victory over the Germans and Sarmatians and his triumph of AD 176. Eleven of these panels survive today, eight of them reused in the Arch of Constantine, with Marcus's head replaced in each panel, and three in the collection of the Museo del Palazzo dei Conservatori in Rome.[19] Whether from one arch or two, and this issue is not relevant here, the panels portray not so much the Marcus as soldier-emperor, seen on the column, as Marcus the good emperor, fulfilling his role in a virtuous manner. The reused and altered panels variously show a *profectio* or departure, a *lustratio* or purification rite, an *adlocutio* or address, a *clementia* or scene of clemency, a scene of submission, the *Rex Datus* scene or installation of a client king, an *adventus* or arrival and a *liberalitas* or giving of bounty. Thus, despite the fact that these panels come from a probable victory monument, there are no scenes of battle represented, nor are there any allusions to the two reported spectacular Weather Miracles with which many people at Rome would have been familiar. Perhaps such scenes occurred on now-lost panels, if such events were portrayed at all. Discussion here will concentrate on two of these panels only, one showing a scene of *clementia* and the other depicting Marcus's triumphal procession through Rome. The static ritualised character of these scenes encapsulates the unchanging ideology of Roman imperial actions, power and rule.

In one of the *clementia* scenes Marcus is pictured in a side-on view, sitting on a stool on a raised dais. A senior officer, probably Claudius Pompeianus, stands behind him, again caught in profile. Both stare ahead, over the heads of a crowd of figures on the ground on which the dais stands. The background figures are all Roman soldiers, four of these being *signifers* or standard bearers. In the foreground are two barbarians, probably Germans. One of them, an elderly bearded man dressed in trousers and a belted tunic, holds out his right arm towards the impassive emperor, seeking clemency, the body of this man being twisted around to partially face the viewer. The old man's other arm is draped around the shoulder of a younger man, a youth really, who is helping to support the weight of the obviously sick or injured older man. Both the old man and the youth, perhaps father and son, display pained expressions on their faces as they await the life-or-death decision of the emperor.

The scene of triumph is one of the simplest compositions to be found on the eleven panels but is all the more powerful for that (*31*). Most of the scene is taken up by the *quadriga,* or four horse chariot, in which Marcus rides. The four upright, proud and beautifully groomed horses trot in overlapping unison, the chariot being accompanied by a *lictor* or magistrate's attendant and a trumpeter. The chariot is caught going through an arch and past a temple in the background of the scene. The decorated chariot carries representations of Roma, Minerva and Neptune, with two flying Victories below. The togate emperor stands at the back of the chariot with Victory hovering behind him with a victor's crown for Marcus's head. The emperor, his original head still intact on this particular panel, stares ahead, a scroll in his hand, looking almost impassive and unmoved by the velocity of the chariot, the sound of the trumpet, the hubbub along the triumphal route and the attentions of the *lictor,* who stares up at him as if in awe and wonder. This would seem more to be the Marcus of the *Meditations* than Marcus the soldier-emperor of the column. It is generally thought that there had originally been a second figure, that of Marcus's son Commodus, riding in the chariot with the emperor on this particular panel, that it portrayed their joint triumph of AD 176, and that the

31 Scene of the emperor in triumph. Panel relief of Marcus Aurelius. Museo del Palazzo dei Conservatori, Rome. (Photo: Author)

panel was subsequently altered to remove Commodus following his murder and *damnatio memoriae*.[20]

A more curious scene of imperial triumph, thought possibly to date to the time of Marcus Aurelius, appears on a ceramic mould from *Aquincum* in *Pannonia*.[21] Probably used for the baking of celebratory cakes, perhaps for state festivals, this object bears decoration conflating military and triumphal events in a manner that suggests the artist's reference to a number of monumental artistic schemes in Rome. The bearded emperor depicted rides in a chariot, shown progressing under a triumphal arch that is heavily decorated with spoils of war in a manner as to suggest its identification as the *Porta Triumphalis* in Rome. The chariot is preceded by the figure of Mars, the god of war. Riding in the chariot with the emperor is Victory, who holds a wreath over his head. While he guides the progress of the chariot with one hand, with the other the emperor thrusts a spear at a bound male barbarian, dressed in tunic and trousers that probably identify him as a German, seated on the ground behind the chariot. Thus battle and triumphal progress are here conflated and the emperor is unusually himself shown in combat with the enemies of the empire, though the symbolic nature of that combat is indicated both by the fact that the barbarian is already bound and defeated and that the emperor fights from a triumphal chariot. If the bearded emperor portrayed on this object was Marcus, then it represents the only extant image of the emperor directly engaged in military action, albeit symbolic action, of the kind that saw Trajan represented as fighting on horseback on both the Great Trajanic Frieze and on the *Tropaeum Traiani* at Adamklissi, as was noted in Chapter Two.

So while scenes of ritual and ritualised conduct dominate the panel reliefs of Marcus, they are also highly significant on the column as well. These rituals were not separate from the conduct of war, but were part of that conduct and therefore ideologically indivisible from it as far as the operation of the army was concerned. Ideology, politics and military imperative functioned together as one thing. These rituals made ideology somehow part of military reality, and vice versa, a process further enhanced through imperial art and architecture.

Away from Rome, Marcus's one-time co-emperor Lucius Verus was celebrated on the Great Antonine Altar at Ephesus, a monument probably erected after his death in AD 169, and celebrating his achievements from his adoption into the imperial family, portrayed in one highly striking scene on the monument, through his military victories against Parthia, to his death and his apotheosis. Some of the battle scenes on the Great Antonine Altar are of a ferocity that up to then was relatively uncommon in Roman imperial art. The use here of these images of extreme Roman violence against barbarian enemies, coupled with an equally gruesome beheading scene on the Bridgeness legionary distance slab from the Antonine Wall in Scotland and dating to the AD 140s, suggest that perhaps such images were first accepted for use in provincial contexts before becoming more mainstream and even more extreme on the Column of Marcus Aurelius in Rome a few decades later.[22]

However, as the Great Antonine Altar was built to honour Verus specifically, rather than to commemorate his joint reign with Marcus, it will not be discussed further here. Parthian men also appear, as captives rather than combatants in this case, on one face of the Arch of Marcus Aurelius and Lucius Verus at Tripoli, another significant provincial Antonine monument.[23] Here the men are in the company of Parthian women and children in family groups posed beneath battle trophies. In the best-preserved of these groups the man stands upright facing out towards the viewer, seemingly alone in contemplation, while the female Parthian sits on the ground at his side and offers comfort to their child, who holds on to her in a return of affection. The barbarian family as a symbol of a whole nation in defeat, used to stress the totality of that defeat, was by now and would continue to be a familiar motif of Roman state art. There was a certain element of pathos and sympathy in the portrayal of the captives on the Tripoli arch which was largely absent from the Great Antonine Altar, the Bridgeness distance slab and the later major Antonine monuments in Rome.

Of course, the single most significant image of Marcus that has come to us is the equestrian statue of the emperor (*32*), the original of which stood for many years in Campidoglio on the Capitoline Hill in Rome and which has now been moved indoors to the Palazzo dei Conservatori and replaced outside in the piazza by a modern copy. Records show that this statue was originally set up in the area of the plaza in front of the Church of St John Lateran.[24]

This bronze, life-size, equestrian statue of Marcus is the only extant example from antiquity of what was a relatively common type of Roman imperial

32 The equestrian statue of Marcus Aurelius in Campidoglio, Rome. (Photo: Author)

representation. Though the equestrian statue derived from a Greek type, it was used in the Roman period in a subtly different manner to demonstrate both individual and state power and authority, rather than simply to honour an individual person, as in the Greek manner. The earliest Roman imperial prototype may have been of Domitian and the influence of the mounted-figure types of Roman military art may have entered the mainstream of state art at this time.

The equestrian Marcus holds one arm and hand in such a position as to suggest that leather reins were originally affixed to the statue and that they were held here, while his other arm is outstretched in a gesture of *clementia*, remarkably similar to his pose on horseback on one of the panel reliefs. The emperor stares straight ahead, rather than at the ground or at any other specific point of reference. The horse is vividly modelled, its mouth open, its mane bristling and its right foreleg either placed on, or trampling, some now-vanished object or person, attested as originally the figure of a cowering barbarian. The overall composition of the statue of Marcus very much reflected the inherent contradictions of his reign, in that here both power and military might were being celebrated in the traditional manner of the trampling of a foe, yet at the same time a generalised gesture of clemency was being extended to the peoples of the barbarian lands. The individual messages of the column and of the arch were here brought together in a powerful way that married the two images of Marcus as philosopher-emperor and soldier-emperor in a highly subtle and successful manner.

4

A Hard Rain

Two of the most striking and memorable images on the Column of Marcus Aurelius are those known collectively as 'The Weather Miracles', that is the so-called 'Miracle of the Thunderbolt', less commonly called 'The Miracle of the Lightning', and 'The Miracle of the Rain' or 'Rains'. The scenes depicting these events occur quite low down on the column (Scenes XI and XVI) and are quite clearly visible to the modern viewer standing in Piazza Colonna today and probably would also have been visible to the contemporary Roman viewer standing on what would have been a lower ground surface at the time. In this chapter an opportunity will be taken to describe and examine these scenes in detail and to try and set them in their historical and legendary context, as well as to consider the broader cultural importance of these scenes to both pagan and Christian Roman viewers.

As was noted in an earlier chapter, the decorated frieze around the column cannot be read as a historical narrative, nor should it be. The design of the frieze was intended to maximise the viewer's engagement with the celebration of Marcus's life through representations of his role during those wars, not to provide a history or narrative of those wars. However, the Weather Miracles represent events both portrayed on the frieze and mentioned in historical sources and therefore they are to some extent unique on the column in this respect and worthy of more detailed analysis here. They certainly stand out from the numerous generic scenes of the emperor sacrificing, the army on the move, battle scenes and so on, that could not with any degree of certainty be linked to recorded historical events, even by the most over-assiduous historian. The Miracle of the Thunderbolt occurs quite low down on the column (Scene XI), soon after the depiction of the crossing of the River Danube, and, though partially damaged, clearly shows a German siege engine being consumed by fire after being struck by a bolt of lightning (33). In the centre of the scene is depicted a Roman stone-walled, crenellated encampment with its wooden fort gates firmly closed against the enemy. Inside can be seen a large number of Roman soldiers crowded together, most of them with their heads turned to view the emperor and his entourage to the right, outside the fort. A few of the soldiers face the other way, to the left, where the German enemy are laying siege to the fort with a siege engine in the form of a wooden tower.

33 Miracle
of the
Thunderbolt.
Scene XI.
The Column
of Marcus
Aurelius, Rome.
(Photo: Graham
Norrie, after
Petersen *et al.*
1896)

To the right, outside the fort, as has been mentioned, stands Marcus, depicted without military uniform and holding an imperial baton. He is surrounded by a bodyguard of legionaries, some of whom are using their shields to provide extra protection for the emperor. It is highly unlikely that Marcus would have put himself in grave danger by leaving his heavily-fortified encampment to engage with the enemy besiegers with only a small force such as this and it is therefore likely that he is depicted in the act of parlaying with the enemy. For the artist, placing the emperor outside the fort, clearly visible in front of his bodyguard may have been a representational strategy to link directly the person of the emperor in the minds of the viewers with events taking place outside the fort, on the side furthest away from the emperor and his entourage. The besiegers, to the left, are depicted at the very moment that a bolt of lightning strikes the wooden siege tower, which they have pushed right up to the walls of the Roman encampment, ready to use it to scale the walls and throw spears and hurl missiles over the parapet at the Roman defenders blockaded inside. The tower would appear to be in the process of collapsing, following the devastating and unexpected lightning strike, while flames can be seen engulfing the upper tiers of the tower. One besieger lies dead on the ground at the base of the tower, thrown down off the tower by the force of the lightning strike, while others appear to be fleeing the scene in abject terror. Immediately after this scene there is a depiction of Marcus sacrificing (Scene XII), which implies that he is here offering up thanks to the gods for their divine intervention in ending the siege.

The Miracle of the Rains again occurs quite low down on the column (Scene XVI) (*34*). The scene is highly complex in terms of the sheer number of figures involved in the action. Roman and German barbarian forces have clearly been ranged in battle order against each other, the Romans to the right and the barbarians to the left, stalemate having been reached between them, as we know from the historical accounts of this battle. We also know, and this will be discussed in more detail below, that the Roman forces have been cut off from any water supply and that the troops and doubtless their cavalry mounts and baggage animals are almost dying of thirst in the burning summer weather. The infantry troops towards the rear of the Roman forces stand stock still, as if awaiting their fate. In the register of figures above them, camp has been struck, as indicated by a tent, while a piece of field artillery mounted on the back of a flat-bed wagon pulled by horses, stands impotently by. There is more movement among the cavalry, while the viewer's eye is suddenly caught by a mêlée of agitated cattle, literally trampling and climbing over in each other, in fear or panic perhaps, as behind them a Roman soldier holds up his right arm to the heavens, either in a plea to the gods above to relieve the drought, or as if he has felt the first tentative drops of the rain that will soon turn into a deluge.

The artist has, however, chosen to depict the moment at which this desperate stand-off is broken by the coming of rains out of the clear blue skies, like manna from heaven; but, most strikingly, he has depicted the rains as emanating from the divine person of an aged male rain god, whose brooding presence and sheer size draws the viewer's eye towards him. Massive in size, with huge wings opened out behind him, he stares out at the viewer with an inscrutable, but troubling, gaze. His long, straggly hair and equally straggly beard merge with the wavy rivulets of rainwater that cascade down from on high. His long arms are outstretched to either side and they, too, are almost hidden by torrents of water sheeting down from heaven to earth. We can see the effects of this welcoming rain on the Roman forces as, almost instantaneously, the soldiers towards the front of the line burst into animated movement. Two of the soldiers hold their shields up in the air, either to fend off the torrential downpour or, more likely, to collect water on the shield surface to quench their debilitating and desperate thirst. Other soldiers, energised by the rain, move into battle against the enemy and there, under the figure of the rain god, we see the aftermath of the Romans' swift, unexpected and obviously devastating attack in the form of a pile of slaughtered bodies of both men and animals, the pile still churning with hints of life. A number of barbarian

34 Miracle of the Rains. Scene XVI. The Column of Marcus Aurelius, Rome. (Photo: Graham Norrie, after Petersen *et al.* 1896)

shields are propped up against this obscene heap, their evident failure to provide much protection against the Roman onslaught having been sadly lamentable.

While the historical sources discussed below attribute the rainstorm to the intervention of *Hermes Aerios* – an Egyptian equivalent to the Roman Mercury – the artist of this scene on the column has chosen, or has been instructed, not to portray the rain god with any attributes such as a *caduceus* or a purse, for example, that would allow his identification as Mercury by the column's viewers, or indeed as any specific Roman deity. He is thus an almost unprecedented divine image in Roman and classical art, an anonymous god, a creation unique to this monument, though certain partial artistic parallels can be found on monuments elsewhere. In Rome the so-called *Bocca della Verita* or Mouth of Truth, a huge, undated circular marble slab that would have probably originally adorned a fountain or other kind of monumental water feature, bears a low-relief representation of an elderly male river god or water deity, whose straggling, water-drenched hair and beard recall the column's rain god in style. On the first-century AD pediment of the temple of Sulis Minerva in Bath appears a bearded, moustachioed male figure with deep-drilled flowing locks of hair and beard, interpreted as a male Medusa, who bears a passing resemblance to the much later rain god on the column.[1]

That these two scenes of divine intervention on behalf of Roman military forces should appear on the column might at first glance suggest that the gods, as always, were on the side of the Romans, and that regular and strict religious observance on the part of the emperor was part and parcel of this symbiotic relationship between Rome and her gods and between Rome and her emperor.[2] Indeed, we have only to look at an earlier scene on the column to see the Roman forces' passage by boat along the River Danube and advance over the Danube bridge being overseen by a benevolent giant river god almost as a matter of course (Scene III). Again, if we look at the decorated frieze around the earlier Trajan's Column, we can once more find a scene in which the god of the Danube appears benevolently (Scene III), another representing a battle in which *Jupiter Tonans*, that is Jupiter the Thunderer, joins in battle on behalf of the Romans, hurling a thunderbolt at the enemy forces (Scene XXIV), perhaps suggesting that a thunderstorm aided the Romans in this battle as well, and a third in which a suggested female personification of night (Scene XXXVIII) provides safe cover for a Roman assault on Dacian forces.

However, there is quite a distinction that can be made between the benevolent overseeing of events, in the person of the river gods on both columns, and the benevolent cover of darkness provided by personified night on Trajan's Column, and the two Weather Miracle interventions on the Column of Marcus Aurelius where the gods helped the Romans avoid disaster through defeat by siege in one case and by drought in another. The gods were not joining in battle simply to aid the Roman forces, as in the case of *Jupiter Tonans* on Trajan's Column, they were stepping in to save them in response to desperate pleas for help. These differences in tone would have been noted by many viewers of the Column of Marcus Aurelius and these scenes may well have stimulated a great deal of heated discussion on Rome's relationship with its pagan gods and, as stories of the Christian God's possible role in events during the frontier wars became more widely circulated, such discussion would have turned to debate about the possible power of this marginal, but outlawed, deity.

History and myth

As has been noted in Chapter One, historical accounts of the Marcomannic wars place such miraculous weather events in the year AD 172, which perhaps suggests that by their placing low down on the column they have been chronologically misplaced in the narrative, given that the first war began in AD 170.[3] If this is so, it may be that the Weather Miracles were such a well known historico-mythological phenomenon or event that viewers would expect to be able easily to pick out their portrayal on the column and would expect to see such important events suitably emphasised in the artwork.

The simplest version of the Miracle of the Thunderbolt is to be found in the *Vita Marci* – the Life of Marcus – in the *Historia Augusta* – the History of the Caesars – a work compiled perhaps in the late fourth century AD. Here it is recounted that the emperor, 'by his prayers summoned a thunderbolt from heaven against a war-engine of the enemy, and successfully besought rain for his men when they were suffering from thirst'.[4] Thus Marcus is directly and unequivocally deemed responsible for the first of the Weather Miracles, which might account for the fact that this version of events, leaving aside a conflation of events in the version of

Dio's History that has come down to us, remained unchallenged and unchanged by subsequent commentators. This was not, in other words, a contested miracle like the Miracle of the Rains was to become. Again, it explains why the emperor personally appears in the representation of the event on the column frieze.

There are a number of differing historical and literary accounts of the Rain Miracle, each of which subtly places a different emphasis on the meaning of this event in terms of its religious or propitious significance and on its links to the emperor's personal qualities. Different named individuals are involved in the invocation of the divine and natural powers to intervene on the Romans' behalf but notably not Marcus himself, apart from in the *Vita Marci* version quoted above. Some accounts view this weather miracle from a purely pagan standpoint, while others give it Christian connotations, though both sides of this argument or schism would appear to agree on the historical veracity of the event, which leads all modern historians to accept that some extreme weather conditions did occur during the war to the advantage of the Roman military forces.

The earliest account of these incidents is given by Cassius Dio in his eighty-book *Roman History*, written in the first quarter of the third century, only a few decades after the events described, an account that appears to conflate the two weather miracles that are depicted as separate incidents on the artwork of the column.[5] It must be remembered, however, that the version of Dio's work that has come down to us is one edited, probably amended and annotated, by an eleventh-century Christian Byzantine monk called John Xiphilinus who may have had his own agenda with regard to presenting the account of these miracles. Dio writes of the problems encountered by Roman forces under Marcus when campaigning against the tribe of the *Quadi* beyond the Danube, and in particular of their blockading by the *Quadi* who had successfully cut off the Romans' access to water supplies. The blockade would appear to have been especially successful given that it was summer and that the scorching sun soon sapped the strength and resolve of the Roman troops, many of whom were either wounded or exhausted by their exertions on campaign. In Dio's words, 'the barbarians were far superior in numbers. The Romans accordingly were in a terrible plight from fatigue, wounds, the heat of the sun, and thirst, and so could neither fight nor retreat, but were standing in line and at their several posts, scorched by the heat'.

Just when the situation seemed to have become critical, with no apparent resolution to benefit the Romans, clouds massed overhead and a massive rainstorm commenced, 'a mighty rain' in the words of Dio, 'not without divine interposition'. Dio relates, 'Indeed, there is a story to the effect that Arnuphis, an Egyptian magician, who was a companion of Marcus, had invoked by means of enchantments various deities and in particular Mercury, the god of the air, and by this means attracted the rain'. He continues:

> at first all turned their faces upwards and received the water in their mouths; then some held out their shields and some their helmets to catch it, and they not only

took deep draughts themselves but also gave their horses to drink. And when the barbarians now charged upon them, they drank and fought at the same time; and some, becoming wounded, actually gulped down the blood that flowed into their helmets, along with the water. So intent, indeed, were most of them on drinking that they would have suffered severely from the enemy's onset, had not a violent hail-storm and numerous thunderbolts fallen upon the ranks of the foe.

Benefitting both from the cooling properties of the rain on their heads and faces and collecting the water to slake their mighty thirsts, the Romans were thus able to repulse this immediate attack on their positions by the *Quadi* warriors, although Dio puts this success down to not only Roman military valour but perhaps more significantly to the increasingly violent weather conditions that had then subsequently escalated into a raging storm of hail and thunder.

In Dio's own words:

thus in one and the same place one might have beheld water and fire descending from the sky simultaneously; so that while those on the one side were being drenched and drinking, the others were being consumed by fire and dying; and while the fire, on the one hand, did not touch the Romans, but, if it fell anywhere among them, was immediately extinguished, the shower, on the other hand, did the barbarians no good, but, like so much oil, actually fed the flames that were consuming them, and they had to search for water even while being drenched with rain. Some wounded themselves in order to quench the fire with their blood, and others rushed over to the side of the Romans, convinced that they alone had the saving water; in any case Marcus took pity on them.

Certain elements of Dio's account, leaving aside his propensity for creating passages of often highly purple prose, particularly the unpleasant aside about the drinking down of enemy blood in the confused frenzy of the battle, curiously mirror the often gratuitously horrific scenes of violence on the column frieze.

The victorious troops then hailed Marcus as *imperator* – emperor – for the seventh time, by this action placing the victory as the responsibility of the emperor and of his relationship with the gods, particularly with *Jupiter Tonans* – The Thunderer. While this acclamation took place in AD 172 it was not until AD 174 that the title of emperor for the seventh time was formally bestowed on Marcus, a discrepancy in dating that has led to some confusion over the date of the Rain Miracle, though a discrepancy which can easily be explained by bureaucratic delays in Rome and the emperor's own extended absences from the capital. Perhaps there was also some initial concern in Rome at news of such an unprecedented event as the reported intervention of the gods in this battle and the acclamation was delayed until details of this remarkable story could be somehow verified. Allowing a story like this to circulate unregulated and uncontrolled could have been dangerous to the Roman state.

It has been argued that the Egyptian magician Arnuphis (sometimes Arnouphis or Harnouphis) mentioned by Dio can be equated with the Arnouphis who dedicated an altar at Aquilea, one of the main urban staging posts for Marcus's army to and from the Danube frontier war zone, thus confirming him to be a real historical figure and not an invented character in Dio's narrative.[6] Evidence of another possible Egyptian connection to the Rain Miracle is suggested by the figure of the god Hermes/Mercury *Aerios* – 'of the air'– a deity to be equated with the native Egyptian deity *Thoth-Shou* and an Egyptian-style temple or *aedicula* on coin issues of AD 172-173 and AD 173-174. These coins bear the unusual legend *RELIG(io) AUG(usti)* which implies some particularly strong link between the emperor and Mercury, who does not otherwise appear on coinage of Marcus's reign, and whose appearance on coins of earlier emperors was relatively uncommon.[7]

However, there are variations on this basic tale. Tertullian, writing towards the end of the second century in AD 197 or 198, attributed the victory to the intervention not of the pagan gods of Rome but to the Christian god:

> Marcus Aurelius too, during his German expedition, succeeded in obtaining rain during that famous drought when the Christian soldiers addressed prayers to God. And when indeed have even droughts failed to be averted by the prayers and fasts of our people? On that occasion the people, acclaiming, 'the God of gods, who alone is mighty', paid tribute to our God under the name of Jupiter.[8]

Over the next two hundred years or so the Christianisation of the Rain Miracle was to be built upon by a number of other writers.

Tertullian placed Marcus Aurelius at the scene of the Rain Miracle, or at least granted the emperor some role in bringing about the miracle, whereas in Dio's account he is simply commander of the forces on campaign, which does not necessarily place him with the blockaded troops: indeed, placing the emperor in a position of peril such as this, even in a literary historical account, might have been seen as overly defeatist. The attribution of the miracle to divine intervention in answer to the soldiers' prayers is again interesting in that it is implied that Christian soldiers' prayers were successful in rousing their one God to intervene on their behalf, thus saving both Christian and pagan soldiers in peril together, while the prayers of the majority pagan soldiers in the beleaguered unit were, so they thought, answered by one of their gods, in this case Jupiter, father of the gods and lord of the elements.

Intriguingly, a series of inscribed altars dedicated to *I(uppiter) O(ptimus) M(aximus) K(arnuntius)*, that is Jupiter the Best and Greatest from *Carnuntum*, has been found at *Carnuntum* which served as Marcus' military headquarters during the Marcomannic wars, the earliest of these dating to AD 172 and placing it in the year of the Weather Miracles.[9] Whether a particularly local variant of Jupiter is attributed here with the saving power of the miracles is uncertain and these altars, like so many others in the Roman world, may simply have been dedicated to the Roman Jupiter.

A third version of the story of the Rain Miracle is provided by Julian the Theurgist, as he is known, or rather by an eleventh-century source who draws upon now-lost accounts of Julian's involvement. Julian was said to have lived at the time of Marcus Aurelius:

> They say about him that once, when the Romans were exhausted by thirst, he suddenly caused dark clouds to gather and discharge torrential rain with incessant thunder and lightning: and that Julian worked this [miracle] by some [secret] wisdom. But others say that Arnouphis, the Egyptian philosopher, worked this wonder.[10]

The Julian story has the air of legend about it, something almost hinted at in the account itself, with the writer telling us the story of Julian's part in the miracle and then, once told, killing the story's likely truth stone dead by bringing up the name of Arnouphis once more. It may be that, in order to counter the Christians' seizing of the Rain Miracle story as an intervention by their God, a story that the involvement of the Egyptian Arnouphis was not strong enough to combat, the pagans had introduced a powerful Chaldaean into the narrative mix at a time when Chaldaeans had become synonomous with divination, dark arts and the occult in general in Late Antiquity.[11]

The Christian version of the story is further Christianised by the church historian Eusebius, bishop of Caesarea, who declared in his *Chronicon* of the late third century that, beset by thirst, legionaries from Melitene knelt down on the ground in prayer to God, much to the amazement of their German foes. The prayers were answered by lightning from the clear blue sky which put the enemy to flight. Heavy rain then came to relieve the plight of the Roman troops without water. Eusebius's work, while clearly assigning the Christian soldiers direct responsibility for invoking this miracle, also indirectly allows Marcus some element of praise by attesting that he gave these Christian soldiers credit for the Rain Miracle.[12]

Just as both pagans and Christians fought over their roles in this contested story for many centuries after the event, so a more contemporary impact was probably created by this tale of supernatural intervention on the remote battlefields on the German frontier as news of the reported event found its way to Rome and around the other provinces of the empire.

Marcus as Jupiter

So far in this analysis of the Weather Miracles represented on the Column of Marcus Aurelius, discussion has concentrated on the Rain Miracle and it has been noted that Cassius Dio's early account of the miracles conflated both events into a single occurrence. However, apart from the column depictions of the Weather Miracles, there is some further independent evidence which surely points to the existence of the Miracle of the Thunderbolt as a separate and distinct event as portrayed on the column frieze. Once more, this corroboration comes from numismatic evidence, consisting of a coin issue of AD 172 which on its obverse bears an image of the emperor in military uniform and holding a thunderbolt as he is crowned by Victory, and also a bronze medallion of Marcus's reign, issued in AD 173, on which is depicted the god Jupiter riding in a *quadriga*, a four-horse chariot, and hurling a thunderbolt at a giant.[13]

It is worth looking outside of Rome at another roughly contemporary monument on which Jupiter and his thunderbolt probably appeared and which, given its contemporaneity to the German wars, might be alluding to the Miracle of the Thunderbolt. Erected in Besançon between AD 172-180, probably in AD 175, the so-called *Porte Noire* or Black Gate (sometimes erroneously called the Arch of Mars) was set up to commemorate the Marcomannic wars (35). The artworks associated with this monument provide an interesting contrast to those on the column in Rome for a number of reasons and have been analysed in detail and published in two comprehensive volumes by Hélène Walter.[14]

Firstly, the analysis of sculptural representations relating to Marcus's German wars from a date contemporary with those wars, as in the case of the Besançon arch, could provide different information about the presentation of that war to the viewers of that time, in comparison to the column's representations of the war which were created almost twenty years later and after the death of Marcus. Secondly, contrasting the style of the sculptural representations on both monuments could prove instructive in terms of comparing metropolitan and provincial art styles, particularly in the light of the significant changes in style attributed, rightly or wrongly, to Marcus's column. Thirdly, and again relating to the metropolitan/ provincial comparison, is the need to question whether the messages promulgated by the artistic programmes on each monument were intended for different audiences of viewers. This is an important line of enquiry that has been successfully followed previously in, for example, comparative analyses of the Augustan monuments of Rome and the contemporary provincial arches of *Gallia Narbonensis* and of Trajanic metropolitan monuments such as Trajan's Column and the Great Trajanic Frieze and the provincial Trajanic trophy monument – the *Tropaeum Traiani* – at Adamklissi in *Moesia Inferior*.[15] Were these messages changed in either style or content, or both, to suit different expected audiences? Finally, there is the central question here as to whether the allusion on the *Porte Noire* at Besançon to the Miracle of the Thunderbolt enhances our understanding of the transmission of the story of this event, or whether a fourth layer of uncertainty is added to the portrayal of this event on the column in Rome, the images of Marcus with a thunderbolt on coin issues of his reign and the multi-layered historical accounts of the incident.

The Besançon arch is a triumphal monument, as opposed to the Column of Marcus Aurelius which, it has been argued elsewhere in this volume, is a funerary monument, albeit with a military-dominated theme and sub-text. Hélène Walter has identified three principal structuring themes for the artistic programme of the arch: the emperor Marcus or Jupiter, the lower world of men, and the upper world of gods and heroes.[16] The interior of the passage through the arch is decorated in

35 The Porte Noire, Besançon. Reconstruction drawing. (Photo: after Walter 1984 Fig. 7)

the tradition of Roman imperial triumphal monuments, with Roman cavalry fighting and defeating eastern barbarians and infantry soldiers doing the same to western barbarians.

The two outer façades of the arch are decorated with an astonishing abundance of figures from Graeco-Roman mythology, presuming a deep and complex knowledge of such matters among the arch's viewers. Many of these figures are linked to myths concerning the punishment of vice of one sort or another, a theme that was often used in Roman art in a contrasting way to highlight the opposed virtues of an individual, in this case the emperor Marcus. On the north face we find depictions of the Labours of Hercules and the myth of Icarus and Dedalus, with figures of Bacchus, Andromeda and the two Dioscuri also being present. On the south face are depictions of Minerva fighting with the giant Enceladus, the madness of Ajax, Alceste and Meleager, Hercules accompanied by the centaur Nessus and Deianeirea, Leda and the swan and Tutela and Eros. On the narrow eastern side we find Ganymede and Jupiter's eagle, Prometheus bound, Hercules and Atlas, and Diana surprised bathing. Also found on the monument are panels depicting captured enemy arms and armour, trophies, as well as captured, chained barbarian prisoners, both male and female. The monument also includes two major figures of Victory in the panel directly over the arched opening, holding swags or garlands between them, and some smaller victories again holding swags.

But it is the decoration in the narrow, curving registers on either side of the keystone that is most relevant here. Portrayed there is a writhing mass of serpentine giants, evidently battling against some foe, an echo of the mortal battles between Romans and barbarians taking place elsewhere on the arch. On the keystone, and thus at the centre of the world, is the position of the badly damaged figure identified as Jupiter. On the reconstruction drawing of the monument he stands upright, holding a spear or thunderbolt in his left hand. To either side of the gigantomachy are triangular panels containing figures of victories trailing garlands or swags between them, further linking with the mythological battle scene and the mortal struggles between Romans and barbarians.

Though there are both western and eastern barbarians depicted on the arch, the conflation of Jupiter with Marcus is by now evident in its allusion to the Miracle of the Thunderbolt from the Marcomannic wars. The appearances of Hercules may well allude to Commodus, son of Marcus, thus also son of Jupiter, particularly if this monument is linked to Marcus and Commodus's joint triumph of AD 176. The point is raised by Walter that Marcus's identification with Jupiter on this monument is part and parcel of a wider phenomenon that encompasses images on medallions, coins, the decoration of cuirass breastplates, and, in particular, Jupiter columns, the latter perhaps also related to the imperial cult in Gaul.

This interesting cultural phenomenon is represented in the German provinces and in the eastern parts of Gaul by the erection of what are known as Jupiter columns or Jupiter-Giant columns, most of these dating to the second or third centuries. These were often sited within temple precincts. Many of these columns were repaired and rededicated around AD 240, events that may have been linked to border raids by the *Alamanni* and their repulsion by Roman forces, suggesting that the columns may have had a political as well as a religious significance.[17]

The Jupiter columns vary in their size and decoration; some are small and relatively simple, others are much larger and quite complex in the iconographic symbolism they bear on their bases and shafts. However, they all share the same general motif that gives the columns their name, in that they have a statue of Jupiter set up on top of the column, the god usually being depicted in the act of riding down a giant usually depicted with serpentine legs. Jupiter is often portrayed in armour and carrying a thunderbolt or thunderbolts. The symbolism is clear: Jupiter/*Taranis*, a syncretism made explicit in inscriptions on some of the column bases, represents the power of Rome and her gods, while the giant represents an enemy of Rome and her gods, probably to be equated with barbarian peoples in general.

While no certain connection can be made in the absence of epigraphic evidence in support of the idea, it is tempting to think that the story of Marcus Aurelius/ Jupiter and the Miracle of the Thunderbolt could have inspired the building of some of the Jupiter columns in Germany and Gaul or have imbued the reading of the iconography of existing columns in the minds of viewers familiar with the legend. To add possible further support to this suggested identification, there are other examples of the overt conflation of Jupiter with Roman military power in Gaul, in the form of two sculptures from Vaison-la-Romaine.[18] The first is a statue of the sky god – Jupiter/*Taranis* – dressed in Roman military armour and holding a wheel and a thunderbolt. He is accompanied by an eagle and a snake. The second sculpture is of Jupiter and Juno together; again, the god wears Roman military garb, carries a wheel and a thunderbolt and is accompanied by an eagle, while Juno appears as a Roman matron accompanied by a peacock and a *patera*. While the date of these two sculptures is uncertain, even if they pre-date the Miracle of the Thunderbolt they nevertheless provide a context in which the pairing of Marcus/Jupiter could become merely an extension of a pre-existing practice of pairing Jupiter/*Taranis* with Roman military power in general.

But to return to the subject of the Weather Miracles, the fact that divine intervention, not once but twice, should have become a leitmotif of the reign of Marcus, need not, therefore, occasion surprise, given that this was a time of remarkable political, military, cultural and religious tension. It would appear that Marcus, by making sure that he was at the heart of the conduct of the state religion, as has been discussed in Chapter Three, was adept at claiming divine sanction for his rule and in so doing diverting any perceived divine wrath that might be thought to be manifested in internal troubles within and outside the empire. The Roman people and the people of the empire more widely at this time were evidently in need of some unconventional way of approaching and connecting with the divine powers, and Marcus apparently found it advisable not to deprive them of this spiritual sustenance during his reign.

The Angel of Mons

Stories of supposedly divine interventions during times of war are not uncommon, but perhaps the most relevant to discuss here is the story of The Angel of Mons from the First World War, given that the creation and enhancement of this rumour into myth is well studied and, as with the Weather Miracles, images of these angels were also created and widely viewed. It is likely that the psychological impact of the Miracle of the Rains on the soldiers present at the battle and on their relatives back home, who would doubtless have heard the story repeated almost endlessly, would have been similar to the impact of the vision or story of the Angel of Mons on British Tommies and their families. While the angels were never monumentalised, their imagined images were widely circulated in newspapers and on postcards, both at the front, and back home in Britain (*36*).

36 'The Angel of Mons' in a contemporary illustration of the First World War. (Photo: the Mary Evans Picture Library)

The origins of this legend, its development and subsequent enhancement have been discussed at length by David Clarke in his book *The Angel of Mons: Phantom Soldiers and Ghostly Guardians.*[19]

The story dates from late August 1914, when the German army was advancing through Mons in Belgium, driving back the British Expeditionary Force into retreat. As with the Roman Rain Miracle, there are many versions of the story, including the form which the angel took or, indeed, in the number of angels intervening on the British side. Phantom bowmen appear in one version, a vision of St George in another. The angels were said to have thrown a protective supernatural cordon around the British troops to ensure their salvation. It has also been suggested that British Intelligence may well have seized upon the gossip and rumours concerning angels circulating among the troops and helped authenticate the tales or at least spread them more widely, in order to boost troop morale at a difficult time. With General Haig's failure to defeat the Germans at Ypres and the first poison gas attacks together depressing British troop morale, there was no more propitious time for angels to intervene on the British side and help raise morale both in the trenches and at home as a result.

Carl Jung was interested in the psychological aspects of this, and other reported sightings, of visions in the sky, encapsulating the flying saucer sightings of the 1950s, and described the Angel of Mons as an example of what he called 'non-pathological' visions or 'visionary rumours'. In David Clarke's words, these:

> had some level of reality to the soldiers who saw it because of their heightened emotional state created by the horror of war. These were to Jung the ideal conditions for a collective vision to manifest itself in the collective mind. The form the vision took was the result of a projection of the conscious or unconscious desires of the subject.[20]

There are, of course, distinct differences between the stories of the Aurelian Weather Miracles and the Angel of Mons. Marcus and Arnuphis are both reported to have prayed for divine intervention, whereas the vision or visions appeared to British troops without first being summoned. The Roman troops are reported to have seen the thunderbolt that struck the siege tower and to have experienced the coming of the deluge of rain but not to have had any vision of a divine figure in association with the sudden extreme weather events. However, there is great similarity in the way that salvation in battle was granted a supernatural or super-normal intervention. There is also similarity in the way that miracle built upon miracle: the Miracle of the Thunderbolt and the Miracle of the Rains perhaps made the soldiers of the Roman army more susceptible to the belief that their saving by the weather was the result of the same phenomenon of divine intervention. The story of the Angel of Mons involves numerous sightings of different visions at different times, all categorised subsequently as being manifestations of the same phenomenon. In both cases the stories or rumours subsequently came to be written down as serious accounts, though the facts of these accounts sometimes became confused, muddled or conflated. Some form of official sanction and manipulation of the stories or rumours took place and artistic representations of the events were eventually made, but only in an ephemeral way with regard to the Angel of Mons. Both stories had a great longevity and both have been claimed for one reason or another by different bodies looking for the validation that association which the stories can provide.

Throughout this book there is constant reference to the viewers of the Column of Marcus Aurelius and much speculation, and speculation it must be, on the reaction of these viewers to certain scenes or messages given out by the artworks of the column, whether these messages were intended or not, and whether they were blatant and overt or subliminal and covert. Indeed, the concept of the primacy of the viewer is now central to the discipline of art history more generally and the focus and motive of the viewer's gaze is endlessly analysed, particularly in matters of sexuality and power differentials. Most writing on the Roman viewer tends to centre on questions of gender, ethnicity and status, as might be expected in a multicultural empire based on military might and slavery. Perhaps the most extraordinary aspect of the story of the Weather Miracles depicted on the Column of Marcus Aurelius is that the scenes could be viewed in a number of different ways, by different viewers, at different periods, depending on whether they were familiar with, or unaware of, the historical or legendary background or backstory and depending on whether they were pagans or Christians, thus introducing a religious element into the viewer's response to the column.

Though the two individual scenes are part of a larger work and would be viewed by many in that broader context, it is likely that the Miracle of the Rains scene might have been viewed out of context by Christian viewers in the later second and third centuries almost as an act of subversion, given the standing of that faith within Rome at that time. It has been suggested that some pagan mythological figures who appear in a number of works of early Christian art, figures such as Orpheus, Bellerophon, Sol, Ulysses and Hercules, were appropriated and thus recontextualised by Christians in these artworks, a process that originally might have begun by the viewing of images of these figures in pagan contexts. Appropriation would therefore first be a mental or psychological act, in the way that it is here suggested Christians might have viewed the Column of Marcus Aurelius because of the inclusion there of the Miracle of the Rains. By claiming these stories as evidence of the power of their God, Christians might also have viewed a monument that clearly depicted such events as their own, Christian, monument right there in the heart of Rome. This would attribute to the column at that time a subversive message that it was never intended to convey. To pagans, before the time of Constantine and the recognition of Christianity as the official religion of the Roman Empire, viewing these scenes might have confirmed their solidarity with an emperor whose due reverence to the gods had resulted in the deliverance of his forces from certain destruction.

5

The Scream

If the Weather Miracles are perhaps the most famous individual images on the Column of Marcus Aurelius, then in terms of its attraction to academics studying the column, the image of a screaming barbarian man in Scene LXVIII is the next most discussed image (37). According to Mary Beard this 'is one of the classic images on the column; often reproduced and often described – in more or less lurid terms'.[1] As she has noted, the screaming barbarian man in this scene, she calls him 'the column's icon', has been previously singled out for particular attention by a number of authorities, in the same way that he is perhaps being singled out here, as being almost emblematic of the message of the monument as a whole.[2]

Beard's caution that isolating individual images such as this can have the effect of destroying discussion of their proper context, which obviously is the context of the artwork of the whole column, is surely well-founded, but that context also includes the situating of his gesture and pose within a range of gestures and poses employed throughout the column's frieze. It is therefore on the screaming man's pose that discussion will concentrate here.

The image of the screaming barbarian man occurs as part of a horrific scene of execution (Scene LXVIII) (38), one of a number of such execution scenes on the column. A group of six Roman footsoldiers, with shields held in one hand and lances in the other, is caught in the act of spearing and killing a number of unarmed barbarian men. One barbarian already lies dead on the ground and another, a man with a long straggly beard, as a spear appears to be thrust deep into his shoulder, lets out a scream of agony that is captured on his face by the artist in a pornography of violence. Being herded towards this killing field (Scene LXIX) are four more male prisoners and a number of barbarian women, two of them holding babies and another touching her young son or daughter who nestles up close to her body. This woman holds one arm protectively across her breast. Whether these men and women are being brought to watch the executions taking place in the adjacent scene or whether they are being led to their own deaths is unclear.

Mary Beard has argued that the screaming man may not in fact be reacting in response to being speared in the back, as I have described above as being the case, and that he may be screaming out or shouting out in horror at his discovery of the dead or dying bodies below him in the foreground of the scene.[3] The spearing in that case, she has argued, is happening in the background, behind him.

37 Close-up view of the screaming barbarian man. Scene LXVIII. The Column of Marcus Aurelius, Rome. (Photo: Graham Norrie, after Petersen *et al.* 1896)

In either case, interpretation is predicated on the understanding that the viewer was, or is, intended to view the screaming man from a frontal position. Beard suggested a second alternative reading of the scene, based on the viewing of the so-called screaming man from the side, in which case, she argued, he appears to be gesturing and shouting out to other barbarians arriving from the left (Scene LXIX). In the same volume of papers in which Beard's readings were presented, Jás Elsner noted that the much-discussed frontality of figures and scenes on the column is actually quite subjective, depending on what angle the viewer looks at any individual scene, for 'the column…. is not a flat but a curved surface',[4] an observation that again might help support the reasoning behind Beard's interesting second alternative reading of the pose of the screaming man.

38 The screaming
barbarian man and other
combatants. Scene LXVIII.
The Column of Marcus
Aurelius, Rome. (Photo:
Graham Norrie, after
Petersen *et al.* 1896)

Scene LXVIII with the screaming barbarian man is positioned on the thirteenth
spiral of the frieze, about two thirds up the column, and can be seen relatively easily
from below in Piazza Colonna by a determined spectator, as the present author noted
on a recent visit. Whether he stood out in any way or was marked out for the benefit
of a second-century viewer of the column is obviously open to question, leaving
aside any painting of the figure that may have originally been done. However, his
unusual pose and gesture, his positioning in high relief almost in the foreground and
at the apex of an almost triangular arrangement of barbarians (one side formed by
bodies to his right, another by the arriving column of men to his left, the third by
the bottom of the spire) suggest that he could have been particularly visible. When
viewed from the ground these compositional elements together also would appear
to argue against his gesture being that of shouting to the men arriving on his left.

The study of the significance of gesture in the visual arts is a well developed
field of academic enquiry, particularly the study of gesture in Roman art.[5]
As might be expected, however, most of the attention of scholars in the field of
Roman gesture has been turned on the Romans themselves and not on others
depicted in Roman visual sources, although many standard poses for mourning
or submissive barbarians have been defined.

The pose of the screaming man on the Aurelian column, when viewed frontally, is striking not only because of the expression on his face and his open mouth, but because of the positioning of his arms, his fully extended right arm being held out from the side of his body, the hand held out flat, palm towards the viewer, with fingers splayed. His left arm is bent at the elbow, with the upper arm held close to the body and the lower arm raised in another open-palmed and splayed-fingered gesture. The classic Roman oratorial gesture for denoting horror involved the speaker turning both of his palms to the left, which would involve him adopting a pose with his left hand more or less identical to that adopted by the screaming man and bringing his right hand across the front of his body.[6] Is the screaming man on the column caught *in stasis*, about to bring his right arm across his body in this way?

Some corner of a foreign field

A second example of a portrayal of a screaming barbarian man occurs in a carved scene on the later second-century tombstone of Caius Septimus of *Legio* I, found at Komarom-Szöny, Roman *Brigetio* in *Pannonia Superior* in modern Hungary, and now in the Magyar Nemzeti Múzeum, Budapest, a depiction which is broadly contemporary with, and remarkably similar to, that of the screaming man on the Column of Marcus Aurelius (*39*).[7]

Unlike the similar screaming man in Scene LXVIII on the Aurelian column discussed above, there can be no doubt about the frontality of the screaming figure on this tombstone and the fact that the viewer would have been expected to position himself or herself central to the stone to view the scene and to read the accompanying inscription. In the scene above the dedicatory inscription, an armed legionary, either Septimus himself or a generic figure of a Roman soldier, stands to the right of a group of barbarian men, with whom he is engaged in combat. One barbarian already lies dead on the ground. A second has fallen to his knees next to him, his body and head turned away from Septimus and almost towards the viewer, his mouth open in a shout or scream. Septimus appears to be reaching out an arm towards him, perhaps to grab his hair with his outstretched hand, before despatching him to the same fate as his fallen comrade, although the stone is quite weathered in this area and Septimus may alternatively simply be gripping a shield with his left hand. A third barbarian combatant moves away from the group to the left. But it is the pain and suffering of the central barbarian protagonist that immediately catches the viewer's gaze and even places the figure of Septimus, the man whose life and career were being celebrated and commemorated here, in an almost supporting role.

The pose and gesturing of the kneeling, screaming man are strikingly similar in some respects to those of the screaming man on the column in Rome. His left arm is similarly bent at the elbow, the upper arm held close against the side

39 Later
second-century
tombstone of
Caius Septimus of
Legio I. (Photo:
Magyar Nemzeti
Múzeum,
Budapest Inv.
Nr.10.1951.102)

of his body, with his lower arm angled away from the body and his left hand
held up in an open-palmed and splayed-fingered gesture, which may represent
either acceptance of the blow about to be struck, or his dismay at the death of
the other barbarian. He looks up to the heavens, mouth agape, with an anguished
expression on his face that catches his suffering in stone for eternity. His fully
extended right arm is held out away from his body at a downward angle, again
in a similar manner to the right arm of the column's screaming man. However,
rather than his hand being open and held palm outwards, the kneeling, screaming
man holds a weapon in his hand in such a way as to suggest that he is about to
loosen his grip on it and let it fall from his hand onto the ground. This provincial
military tombstone and its imagery caught the attention of Ranuccio Bianchi
Bandinelli who discussed it as an example of an early trend towards the kind of
simplified, frontally composed imagery that became typical in the art styles of
Late Antiquity,[8] but he did not consider the significance of the protagonists' poses
and gestures in detail, or place them in a broader context of the portrayal of pain
and suffering in classical art and the significance of such portrayals.

It must be asked whether any of the numerous images of suffering barbarians, like the two images of screaming men under discussion in this chapter, or mutilated barbarian bodies on the Column of Marcus Aurelius and the Bridgeness legionary distance slab from the Antonine Wall in Scotland,[9] for instance, were linked to the broader use of pornographic or sexually violent iconography in Roman culture. Was there some element of sadism or voyeurism inherent in the creation of these depictions and in their viewing by different ancient audiences? Was the use of such images a cynical process linked to political expediency in the Antonine period? Consideration of a number of other artworks of the time suggests that in all three areas this might have been the case.

While Laura Mulvey's theories of the gaze have been hugely influential on the discipline of art history, it is only relatively recently that these have been widely applied to the Roman period.[10] However, some years earlier Carlin Barton considered issues relating to the figure of the gladiator using the theory of the gaze and other, psychoanalytical frameworks of analysis, centring the gladiator at the heart of a web of what she saw as institutionalised sadomasochistic violence endemic in Roman culture.[11]

Mythological suffering

There are certainly a number of earlier possible iconographic models for the Roman screaming men, something which might serve to place them in an artistic lineage that has nothing to do with Roman voyeurism. Canonical Hellenistic Greek images of screaming men include the so-called Laocoon Group in the Vatican Museums, a work in the Hellenistic Baroque style and dating from some time between the second century BC to the first century AD, and some of the figures of giants battling with gods and goddesses on the frieze of the Altar of Zeus at Pergamon, a work dating to *c.*170 BC. These works would have been widely known and admired in the Roman world and thus the knowledge of such images may have had some influence on the use of the image of the screaming man on the Column of Marcus Aurelius. However, it might be considered to have been a particularly significant conceptual leap for the Roman artists to have portrayed badly suffering contemporary human enemies, rather than suffering mythological figures.

The common Graeco-Roman sculptural subject of the punishment of the satyr Marsyas,[12] who had the temerity or, in retrospect, the foolishness to challenge Apollo to a musical contest, could be seen as belonging to a strain of images in classical art which portray suffering in a voyeuristic manner, though the subject matter in this case was once more purely mythological. Having lost the musical contest, Marsyas had to submit himself to Apollo's chosen forfeit, for the satyr to be flayed alive by his Scythian servant.

While pre-Hellenistic representations of this story generally concentrated on the musical contest, leaving the appalling aftermath to the imagination of

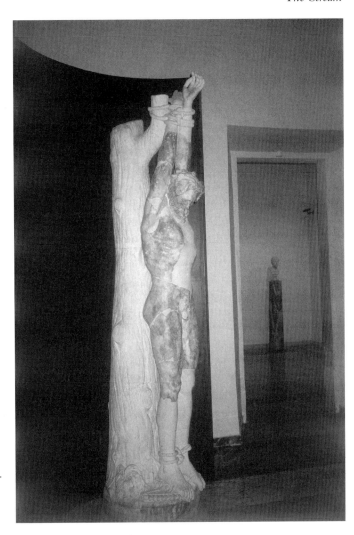

40 The Hanging Marsyas.
Museo del Palazzo dei
Conservatori, Rome.
(Photo: Author)

the viewers, Hellenistic and Roman sculptures, perhaps all derived from the Hellenistic original of the mid-third century BC known today as the *Hanging Marsyas*, depicted the distressed and anguished Marsyas strung up in a tree, hanging by his hands, positioned above and behind his head, and awaiting the cut of the Scythian's knife (*40*). He hangs his head down, his face apprehensive, but otherwise unresponsive: there is no mask of pain, no scream. Pliny tells us that visitors would be taken to a particular plane tree in Phrygia where Marsyas was said to have been punished in this way by the god Apollo, something that clearly demonstrates the power, popularity and dark voyeuristic lure of this particularly grotesque myth. Gazing upon both the terrible suffering of Marsyas and on the suffering of a screaming barbarian enemy of Rome may have provided a vicarious thrill for some viewers whose psyches were perhaps conditioned to deal with the broader acceptance of violent imagery in Roman culture and society.

Violent entertainments

The regular, ingrained use of violent imagery in the Latin language, in Roman literature and in the visual arts of the period, including the more demotic art of *graffiti* caricature, situated the commonly used images of suffering and of defeated barbarian enemies of Rome within a broader framework of violence and conflict within Roman society. Most obviously this institutionalised violence was manifested in the actuality of the violence of the games in the arena and in certain aspects of judicial punishment. Theatricality and the use of striking imagery played their part in these aspects of Roman life too.[13]

A formal link between the captive barbarian and the gladiatorial system is shown by Cicero's assertion that in his time the gladiators were 'either debased men or foreigners', the latter in most cases having been brought to Rome for this express purpose. Gladiatorial combats even became part of the celebration of conquests and formal triumphs in Rome and, for instance, on the occasion of the celebration of his Dacian victory, the emperor Trajan sponsored an extended series of gladiatorial contests, involving ten thousand combatants engaged in the arena over a period of four months.[14]

Even allowing for literary licence in the reporting of the numbers involved, the scale of such organised and ritualised slaughter was probably considerable. That it was linked not to the formalised slaughter of war, but rather to peace in the aftermath of war, seems perhaps both contradictory and confusing to the modern mind. The gladiatorial events and the events of war were here conflated to become metaphorical signifiers of the potential power inherent in the Roman state's control over the process of even death itself. Both events, in order for them to be rationalised within the Roman psyche as being an integral part of the same cultural matrix that found space for the writings of Cicero and the wall paintings of Pompeii, may have originally relied on the concept that without an equal opponent there could be no celebration of valour. Later, observing suffering may have become almost an end in itself for the spectators at the games. Cicero had already lamented in 52 BC how unsympathetic many Roman viewers were for those defeated, killed or humiliated in the arena.[15]

It would also seem to be the case that the imagery of victory in general, incorporating the barbarian captive, was appropriated in the context of the ritual and celebration of gladiatorial games. This was perhaps in the same way that in the later empire the iconography of imperial victory, particularly on the so-called consular diptychs, was extended by the adoption of depictions of victory in the arena or the circus as being more widely symbolic in political and military terms.

Just as images of defeated or suffering barbarians were widespread in Roman art, so too were images of death in the arena and of other violent acts, even in domestic settings. Just as these images of barbarians could be particularly graphic or extreme, as in the case of the image of a screaming male barbarian on the Column of Marcus Aurelius which forms the subject of this chapter, so too could be some images of the games. This is well demonstrated by a particularly gruesome example of a beheading scene during a gladiatorial combat on a relief from Due Madonne, Bologna, dated to the second half of the first century BC (*41*). On the right of the surviving part of the relief is a gladiator with raised right arm looking to strike at an opponent who must have appeared on the now-missing part of the relief. But it is the scene on the left-hand side of the stone that is of relevance here. A third gladiator, clad in a short skirt-like garment held in place with a thick belt, boots, a wrist-guard and a helmet, holds up an oval shield in his left hand and moves his right, sword hand down towards his waist, having just struck a swingeing blow to behead a fourth gladiator who kneels on the ground to his right. The kneeling figure, hands held passively behind his back, is headless. His head, still encased in his helmet, falls to the ground to his right, his shield discarded behind him. Here, once more, a human body is being turned into disassociated, dehumanised fragments.

The arena was inextricably linked with the Roman system of judicial punishment, with condemned criminals often featuring in the arena in extraordinary mythological enactments or tableaux that led inevitably to their deaths there. The subject of Roman judicial savagery in general has been considered by Ramsay MacMullen who has noted that the number of crimes for which capital punishment was to be meted out, rose considerably in the period after AD 200, although savage punishment involving disfiguring of the body was relatively common before this date.[16]

After AD 200 some crimes that had previously merited decapitation now were subjected to supposedly harsher punishments such as 'crucifixion, burning, or wild beasts',[17] something that perhaps is mirrored by the increasingly dehumanised images of suffering barbarians in Roman art from the later second century onwards. The fragmentation of bodies in art is mirrored by judicial overseeing of the fragmenting of real criminal bodies: Eusebius' accounts of the judicial mutilation of Christians by the breaking of legs, the cutting out of an Achilles tendon, the putting out of an eye or the cutting off of an ear or the nose are particularly revealing in this respect.[18] Under Constantine some corrupt officials could have their hands amputated, punishment also recorded as commonplace under Valentinian and in the army under Theodosius, though mutilation was not a formal judicial penalty before AD 300. 'Amputation, whether loss of a foot for a deserter, of a hand for the destroyer of public buildings, or of sexual organs for the pederast (under Justinian)', proclaimed 'symbolically the particular evil being punished'.[19]

It can be argued, therefore, that rather than the violent images on such monuments as the Column of Marcus Aurelius, being understandable only within the context of the monument itself and of its programme of decoration, they need to be seen, along with all violent images of the time, within the

41 Relief depicting gladiatorial combat from Due Madonne, Bologna. Museo Civico
Archeologico di Bologna. (Photo: Author)

context of the regular, institutionalised manifestation of violence in certain areas
of Roman society, including the games and violent judicial punishment. More
broadly still, perhaps Roman images of violence created for political ends need
to be analysed in terms of a general history of the depiction of conflict, pain, and
suffering.[20]

There is a considerable and growing art historical literature on the representation
of pain and suffering, of violence against the individual, in medieval and more
recent art, a reading of which has aided the construction of the thesis of this
present discussion of screaming barbarians in Roman art. Images of pain and
suffering in Roman art and literature often have otherwise tended to be discussed
only in the context of the cultures of the classical world and the reception of its
myths, literature and art in later periods. Studies consulted during research for
this book include analyses of gestures of despair in medieval and Renaissance art,
of representations of punishment in the Florentine Renaissance, of crucifixions,
of the image of the severed head, principally in the art of Gericault, of war as
depicted by Callot and Goya, of pain, violence and martyrdom, and of medieval
martyr pictures in particular.[21]

A modern conditioning

These studies of the longer-term history of depictions of pain and suffering might be argued to illustrate how modern attitudes to such images can condition the response of present-day observers to older images, such as those of the Roman and medieval periods; how, in fact, it might be easier to condemn the use of such images rather than try to understand them in their contemporary context. On the other hand, it might be that the embedding of violent Roman images in an analysis of violent images in general allows them to be analysed in terms of the widespread aestheticisation of pain for political or religious purposes. Likewise, it could be that our familiarity with a number of what are generally viewed as iconic images of suffering in twentieth-century art and photojournalism can prejudice our viewing of earlier images, although once more perhaps stronger arguments for their relevance to a study such as this can be put forward.

The art historian Richard Brilliant has interestingly recorded how in the 1960s, 'at a time of considerable unrest on American campuses because of opposition to the Vietnam War by students and faculty', he met students' requests to speak about the war by lecturing on Marcus's Germanic wars:

> using details [of the column frieze] taken photographically, often in close-up, of the more savage scenes of killing, pillaging, burning, the slaughter of captives, and the taking of women and children into captivity or slavery; Vietnam was never mentioned, but the audience fully understood the subtext of my lecture, and responded in sympathy, sadness, and with tears to the gestural situations presented to them, which they immediately comprehended. Perhaps these scenes have a universality of response because empathy is so much a part of our *humanitas*.[22]

While he does not record whether the image of the screaming barbarian man was one of these close-up images, given his 'iconic status' it is likely that it was.

Discussion of images of screaming people would not seem to be complete without at least a mention of Edvard Munch's 1893 painting *The Scream*, a work that exists in a number of versions, and a number of works by Francis Bacon, of which the so-called 'Screaming Pope' or, more properly, *Study After Velásquez's Portrait of Pope Innocent X* of 1953 is probably the most relevant here. But these modern iconic images are not related to artistic explorations of political or religious conflict or of suffering in war. However, the very existence of these works – and particularly their widespread dissemination today through their reproduction – might almost be thought to pre-judge discussion of other screaming images. As Munch himself wrote about his most famous painting, the male protagonist of the picture is, 'trembling with anxiety ... [as he felt] ...a great, infinite scream pass through nature'.[23] In other words the painting's open-mouthed human subject is reacting to an inner scream.

Less reproduced, and of more relevance to the discussion here of the depiction of pain and suffering in wartime, is Mark Gertler's painting *The Merry-Go-Round*, painted in 1916 and now in the collection of the Tate Gallery, London (*42*).[24] This is one of the most powerful British pictures of the First World War. Highly allusive, the picture is of an almost folk-art-like merry-go-round ride, the rides themselves being closely packed trios of white horses. The riders, almost doll or puppet-like, are a mixed group of men, women, and one child. Most of the men are in uniform, either blue naval or bright red army parade dress. The faces of all the riders can be seen by the viewer, either full-on in the case of one of the groups of riders, or from the side in the other four groups. A solitary uniformed rider on the right hand side of the picture has his back to the viewer. All the riders' mouths are wide open in a scream or a shout as stylised storm clouds gather over and behind the orange-red canopy of the merry-go-round and as the horses rotate, a reflection that the First World War was gathering pace and that British casualties were increasing dramatically. A photographic reproduction of the picture was described at the time by D.H. Lawrence in an appreciative letter to Gertler as being '[of] the best modern picture I have seen: I think it is great and true, but it is horrible and terrifying'.[25]

In the later twentieth century a screaming figure likewise became almost the iconic image of the Vietnam War, when in 1972 Nick Ut, an Associated Press

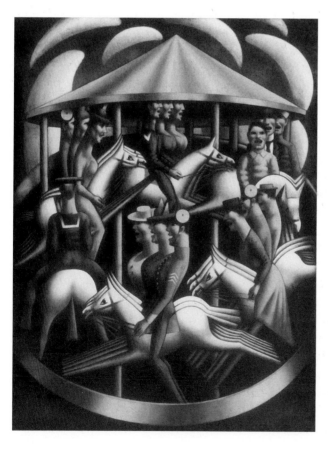

42 *The Merry-Go-Round* by Mark Gertler, 1916. Tate Gallery, London. (Photo: copyright Tate, London 2005)

photographer, took a picture of a group of Vietnamese children running down a road after a napalm attack, the viewer's attention being drawn to nine-year-old Phan Thi Kim Phuc who had torn off all of her burning clothing and who was running naked, arms outstretched and screaming down the road with her companions. Ut's black-and-white photograph was carried by newspapers across the world and has been endlessly anthologised and reproduced ever since: its publication indeed was a powerful incentive to the growth of the anti-war lobby worldwide. Equally significantly, or indeed more importantly, Ut did not see himself simply as a documentarist or chronicler of suffering, and immediately after taking the photograph he caught up with Phan Thi Kim Phuc and drove her to the nearest hospital, an hour's drive away.

Even more recently, in September 2004, of the many horrific images to come out of the Chechen militants' seizure of Beslan Middle School Number One, North Ossetia, and the bloody end to the siege there, perhaps the most alarmingly representative was taken by Sergei Dolzhenko of EPA. His colour photograph shows two un-named children, a boy and a girl in the foreground, with adult victims lying or sitting on stretchers in the background. The boy and girl are naked, apart from dirty and bloodstained underpants, the girl stands to the right of the picture with her back to the camera, while the boy, probably only seven or eight years of age, stands to the left and looks straight at the lens/viewer. He is slightly hunched forward, with his arms held in at his sides and his hands held out in front of him, the fingers clenched. His face is contorted with fear and shock and his mouth is open in a scream or howling cry.

When created, the Roman images of screaming men which form the subject of this chapter might have evoked for some knowledgeable, contemporary viewers allusions to well-known depictions of suffering mythological figures, such as the screaming giants at Pergamon or the screaming Laocoon, thus possibly diminishing or eliminating the viewers' empathy for what were really images of suffering contemporary human enemies. It may be that our modern eyes are drawn to these extraordinary Roman images and our minds to empathising or sympathising with them because of all the mental baggage we carry in the form of familiarity with the screaming images of Munch, Bacon, and Gertler, or, more tellingly, of real suffering children in photographs of Vietnam or North Ossetia. Perhaps familiarity with these modern images enhances but conditions the interpretation of the Roman images.

Academic studies of the Roman army have recently been criticised for not confronting or dealing with the issue of violence and suffering in warfare alongside studies of army structure and organisation, battle tactics and campaigns, the morphology of camps and frontiers, and military equipment,[26] although the link between the Roman army and morality in warfare is an important topic that has been considered recently by one authority.[27] But to find detailed and theoretically-informed studies of warfare as a culturally-embedded phenomenon, to construct an anthropology of violence and to view conflict in a wider framework it is necessary to look at academic studies of other chronological periods and of other cultures.[28] To find analyses of the cultural history of depicting pain and suffering it is necessary to look again outside the field of purely classical scholarship to art-historical studies such as those discussed in detail above.

The study of artworks commemorating Roman imperial triumph and the exploits and achievements of the army need to be viewed within the context of studies of institutionalised violence in Roman society both in the Republican and Imperial periods, and of the whole process of *damnatio memoriae* which was itself part and parcel of a process of violence against certain individuals, their images and their memory and which was testimony to the power and potency of visual imagery in Roman society.

The two images of screaming male barbarians discussed in detail in this chapter are both signifiers of the power of Rome and of the horrors of war. As these two particular images are extremely unusual both in their individual contexts of use and more broadly in the overall context of Roman images of barbarian enemies they act to draw in the modern viewer's eye. In the case of the barbarian on Septimus's tombstone he almost seems to become the subject of the composition. By being such powerful images, to the ancient viewer they may have stressed not only Rome's power but also its ruthlessness in necessity. In manipulating images of evident pain and suffering in the service of political art, an aesthetic of violence was created that makes it difficult to accept the interpretation that it was also the humanity of their barbarian enemies that was being evoked for the ancient viewer when invited to look upon these images of pain and suffering.

It could be argued that on the Column of Marcus Aurelius and on the Septimus tombstone the barbarian had simply become a body; dehumanised pieces and fragments of bleeding and battered flesh, whose fate was dictated by Roman imperial authority. On the column these bodies were stabbed or hacked at, pushed and herded like beasts being brought in from the fields, pulled along by the hair, beheaded, and their bodies piled up in heaps for the edification of the Roman viewers. The two images of screaming barbarian men represent not only significant examples of a pornography of political violence in Roman society in the Antonine period, but also examples in a sadly more extended line of depictions of those who suffer in conflict.

Power and Gender

Recently a great deal of attention has been paid by various scholars, including the present writer, to the appearance of a single eroticised image of the goddess Victory and numerous images of mortal, barbarian women on the Column of Marcus Aurelius. Victory also appeared on Trajan's Column, quite naturally it might be assumed in the context of celebrating Roman victory in war, but the Aurelian image of Victory is altogether different, as will be discussed in detail below. Unlike Trajan's Column, on which numbers of non-barbarian, though non-Roman, women appear, it is only barbarian women that appear on Marcus's column, often in scenes where they are depicted as victims of violence at the hands of Roman soldiers. Why should this be so and what does it tell us about Roman attitudes to these women and about the relationship between male Roman victors and conquerors and the female barbarian defeated? The issue of violence against women as portrayed on the column is dealt with here at length as it perhaps provides an insight into the Roman male imperial psyche.

Mother of the Camps, erotic Victory

Despite the fact that in antiquity the Column of Marcus Aurelius, as we call it today, might have been known as the Column of (Divine) Marcus Aurelius and Faustina, the empress Faustina appears nowhere on the column nor, as far as we know, on its original decorated base. It has been suggested that her statue, along with that of Marcus, could have adorned the top of the column, but most commentators assume that only Marcus was represented by a statue here.[1] Omitting Faustina would be very much in keeping with the ethos of the artworks on the column, that it was a soldier-emperor being memorialised here by Commodus and not a family man, although the two roles would not necessarily have been viewed as being mutually exclusive. Faustina did, in fact, accompany Marcus on campaign in both wars in the west and in the east, dying at the end of the war in the east in AD 175.

Yet the Antonine dynasty was one in which the strength of the idea of family lineage was important, best illustrated by the way in which the elder Faustina, wife of Antoninus Pius and mother of the younger Faustina who married Marcus, was celebrated after her death. Not only does she appear in the apotheosis scene on the decorated base of the Column of Antoninus Pius, erected by Marcus and Lucius Verus, but she continued to be represented and named on Pius's coinage, 'more often than is the case with any other member of the imperial family after death'.[2] For Commodus, to have celebrated the younger Faustina, his mother, along with his father Marcus on the column would have been in keeping with this new dynastic tradition. It was not the case that images of Faustina would have been out of place in the context of the depiction of manly military endeavours, for she did campaign with Marcus and she was the first empress to be given the title of *Mater Castrorum* – Mother of the Camps – a title that saluted her links with the army established while she was on campaign with Marcus and which appeared alongside her name on a number of coin issues, though it is not attested on inscriptions.[3] It has been suggested that Faustina may be represented as *Mater Castrorum* in the *adventus* scene on one of the Aurelian panel reliefs.[4]

It is possible that the figure of Victory on the Column of Marcus Aurelius, and indeed the victory who crowns Marcus in his chariot on one of the Aurelian panel reliefs, could have been conflated in the artist's eye and the knowledgeable viewer's mind, with the person of Faustina. The fact that Victory on the column appears on the north-east face where Marcus first appears and that the emperor's appearances link together vertically, it may be that Victory/Faustina was intended to be part of this enchainment. There can be found a number of instances in which imperial women appear in contexts where they are portrayed as Victory and, indeed, there are Antonine links with the goddess, in that the temple dedicated to Antoninus Pius and Faustina the elder after their deaths bore victories set as corner *akroteria*. It has even been suggested that Faustina the Elder is the female figure portrayed on the Hutcheson Hill legionary distance slab from the Antonine Wall in Scotland, awarding a wreath to the victorious Roman troops, possibly in the guise of Victory, but more probably as *Divus Faustina* – Divine Faustina.[5] Julia Domna, wife of Septimius Severus, was portrayed in the early third century as a winged victory on a cameo from Kassel and as a wingless victory crowning Caracalla with a laurel wreath on a decorated relief, now in a Polish collection, indicating that this practice of conflating Victory and empress extended beyond the Antonine period.[6]

The figure of Victory on the column appears almost exactly half way up the shaft in Scene LV, her appearance marking the end of the first phase of the wars in or around AD 176 (*43*). She is depicted as a giant figure, all the better for the viewers below to see this important deity here. She is flanked by two battlefield trophies, trees hung with captured barbarian arms and armour and with stacks of shields at their bases. She is depicted in the act of writing upon a huge oval shield the details of the victory being celebrated and commemorated, but any inscription the shield's surface may originally have borne has now worn off through weathering. As has been pointed out by a number of authorities, the figure of Victory used here is a standard classical female type modelled on the Greek Aphrodite of Capua, her forward-leaning pose and her semi-naked

state – she is partially draped over her upper body by a robe which falls away
to also reveal part of her upper thigh – adding a frisson of sexual tension to
the testosterone-powered images that dominate the column frieze.[7] Her closest
parallel, and this is hardly surprising given the close links between the two
columns, is the Victory on Trajan's Column, again portrayed inscribing some
words on a noticeably much smaller shield.[8] This Trajanic Victory is almost fully
clothed, in contrast to the Aurelian Victory and it must be asked whether there is
some particular significance in this marked difference.

Detailed comparison of the two Victory figures shows that there are other
more subtle differences as well. The Trajanic Victory's small shield, wreathed with
laurel, rested on a low pillar, and she herself is shown with her left foot standing
on a discarded military helmet. On the Aurelian column there is no pillar, possibly
omitted to allow for the employment of a more sizeable shield bearing a larger,
more visible inscription, and no helmet beneath Victory's foot.

43 An
eroticised
Victory.
Scene LV–LVL
The Column
of Marcus
Aurelius, Rome.
(Photo: Graham
Norrie, after
Petersen *et al.*
1896)

It is of great interest here to note that a popular Antonine statuary theme was the depiction of mortal married couples as Mars and Venus, the latter the Roman equivalent of the Greek Aphrodite, with the Venus/wife figure sometimes modelled on the Aphrodite of Capua, in order 'to praise the wife's beauty, desirability, and love for her husband'.[9] It may follow, therefore, that the erotic Victory/Venus on the Aurelian Column could have been equated with Faustina in just such a manner, while the soldier-emperor guise for Marcus, attributed to him on the column frieze, could have equated him in the viewer's eyes with Mars. Along with the suggested links between Faustina and other imperial women with Victory, then such an interpretation may be correct. This would, however, raise some issues about the relationship of a son who would sanction his parents' depiction in this way, particularly the eroticisation of his mother through the promulgation of such a seductive public image.

It is difficult to agree with the interpretation that the Aurelian Victory was a symbol of the Roman spreading of *humanitas* through conquest, and that, as one recent commentator has written, 'her erotic appearance intimated that Roman victory, and the civilisation it brought, were attractive to both the conquerors and the conquered' and that she 'served to convey an idealised view of Roman imperialism as a civilizing mission'.[10] While such strategies might well have been applicable as ways of putting the Roman imperial message across in the era up to and including the emperors Trajan and Hadrian, by the time of Commodus that message would have appeared overly simplistic and not fit for the times. Marcus was not seeking to expand the empire in the way that emperors from Augustus to Trajan had been doing, he was fighting what was, to all intents and purposes, a desperate defensive war. Individual elements can be pulled out of the context of an overall monument for analysis, as in this volume, but this must not be done in a blinkered manner that ignores the desperate scenes of carnage which dominate the Aurelian column and which bring into question the very idea of the wars against the Germans being somehow part of a civilizing mission on behalf of the Romans.

Women on the column

Numerous images of mortal women also appear on the column, all of them barbarian women. Many of these barbarian women are mothers and the interaction between these mothers and their children and between some of these mothers and Roman soldiers is often portrayed in quite fraught images of violence and of the threat of impending violence.[11]

The first question to consider is why so many images of women appear on the column? The point has been made elsewhere in this volume that the repetition of certain kinds of images in order to stress their significance is part of the clear programmatic design of the column frieze, intended perhaps to inculcate that message to the viewer who noticed repeated images. The most repeated images are those of the emperor himself, the Roman army successful in battle, the barbarians defeated in battle, the linking of the gods to the success of Roman endeavours in the form of a river god, the Weather Miracles and Victory, architectural motifs denoting either civilization or barbarity, and images of Roman violence against barbarian women. Thus repetition increases the number of images, but it also highlights their individual importance in the overall programmatic scheme.

The second question to address is whether this portrayal of Roman violence against women is out of the ordinary. The answer to this must be both yes and no. Yes, because no other single monument, either earlier or later, in Rome or in the provinces of the empire, can be cited as a parallel for such an intensive use of images of barbarian women suffering from Roman military violence. No, because a number of individual images of barbarian women suffering violence can be found in Roman art; indeed, the so-called mourning-captive motif of a captured, grieving barbarian woman or of a captured, either bound or unbound barbarian woman, sitting at the base of a trophy, normally in a pair with a bound male barbarian, are extremely common on both Roman monuments and coinage.[12]

The most noteworthy individual violent motifs pre-dating the Column of Marcus Aurelius occur on the *Gemma Augustea*, an Augustan court cameo, where the so-called hair-pulling motif is employed in the depiction of a barbarian woman being pulled along by the hair by a Roman soldier,[13] and on the Claudius and *Britannia* carving from the *Sebasteion* or temple to the Julio-Claudian cult at Aphrodisias in Asia Minor, where a highly eroticised and sexually charged scene depicts the heroically naked emperor battering a partly naked female personification of the conquered province (44).[14] While at one stage there was a tendency for photographs of this image to be used simply as an illustration of the Roman conquest of Britain, without comment on the nature of the scene depicted, it is now more widely discussed as an image of extreme male violence against women and as a metaphor for Roman male imperial ideology as it encompassed the position and status of conquered or captured women.

Before further discussing this issue, the opportunity will be taken to describe here in detail a number of individual scenes involving women on the column, including depictions of violence against them. These scenes can be divided up into four categories, the first being scenes of actual physical violence against barbarian women, including the killing of some women, the second being a scene of the aftermath of a possible rape or sexual assault, the third being scenes involving the physical manhandling of women and children or their mistreatment as they are taken prisoner, and the fourth and final category being scenes of women in captivity and their transporting away from the area, presumably into slavery in Rome and elsewhere.

There are two definite instances of the depiction of barbarian women being killed (Scene xcvii) (45). In this scene, following a battle, a woman is dragged off by the hair, a motif that was employed in other scenes and which will be discussed below, and her child is led away by two Roman soldiers. Behind them skirmishing

44 Claudius
and Britannia.
The Sebasteion,
Aphrodisias.
(Drawing by
Mark Breedon)

Roman troops have knocked a barbarian woman to the ground. Although this
figure is badly damaged and the carving is missing its head, it would appear that
she is caught in the act of being struck down, her arms outstretched, her thin
dress clinging around her legs as she falls. Ahead of the woman being dragged by
her hair walks another woman with her Roman captors, her head bowed and
her arms down at her sides, the Roman soldier behind her firmly holding on
to her right arm with his right hand, as if to forcibly move her forward. In the
background of this scene, in the upper register, another Roman soldier appears to
rush at a female barbarian and stab her in the breast with his sword as she attempts
to raise up one of her arms in futile self-defence, her other arm hanging loose
by her side, her hand held out tensely from her side. Another Roman trooper
passively looks back at this bloody scene in the only acknowledgement of its
occurrence on the column. The killing of these two barbarian women is shocking
in its ferocity and understatement and perhaps also surprising, given that captured
women would have been valuable to the Romans as slaves.

45 Violence against female barbarians. Scene XCVII. The Column of Marcus Aurelius, Rome.
(Photo: Graham Norrie, after Petersen *et al.* 1896)

There is a third possible killing scene, although in this instance the actual killer blow is not depicted as it happens; rather, it would appear to be about to be struck. The scene is of the sacking of a German village (Scene XLIII) by Roman infantry and cavalry troops (*46*). As the cavalrymen ride through the village a German woman either emerges from a hut and starts to run for her life, or she is depicted running past the hut door. Ahead of her are Roman cavalrymen who have already made their first sweep through the village at a gallop, behind her come Roman footsoldiers mopping up opposition. One of the Roman cavalrymen in the upper register that forms the background of the scene is shown in the action of raising his lance as if about to spear the fleeing barbarian woman in the foreground, or at least to scare her by his actions. It is uncertain, however, whether these two figures are meant to be in the same field of activity. The depiction of this terrified woman is unusual in another way, in that her robe is depicted as being almost diaphanous, clinging to her legs and hips as she runs for her life, and the material billowing with her movements. The image is almost that of an eroticised dancer, perhaps a Maenad, rather than a victim of war.

The scene that possibly shows the aftermath of a rape (Scene CII) occurs towards the top of the column, in a composition that is centred on the portrayal of the destruction and burning of a German village (*47*). As huts are set ablaze by

46 The sacking of a German village. Scene XLIII. The Column of Marcus Aurelius, Rome. (Photo: Graham Norrie, after Petersen *et al.* 1896)

a Roman soldier holding a flaming torch, other soldiers proceed to capture, bind and lead away the men of the village. On the right-hand side of the scene stands the solitary figure of a woman holding the shoulder of a small girl standing at her feet. The woman's dress is pulled completely off her shoulders and her upper body is exposed and naked. With her other hand she is holding up her ripped dress and has managed to bring it up sufficiently to cover her breasts and secure some modesty. It is difficult not to view this woman as the victim of a sexual assault by one of the Roman soldiers sacking the village. Here, the rape of the woman is being equated with the rape of her people by the Romans and the rape of their village and homeland.

Scenes involving the physical manhandling of women and children or their mistreatment are more numerous than killing scenes, and include hair-pulling scenes as well as more general depictions of mistreatment. Hair-pulling scenes

47 The sacking of a German village and the probable aftermath of a rape. Scene CII. The Column of Marcus Aurelius, Rome. (Photo: Graham Norrie, after Petersen *et al.* 1896)

occur at least twice, one of these scenes (Scene XCVII) already having been described. The second instance (Scene XX) occurs during the sacking of a German village, with the emperor and his attendant officers being shown as spectators at the event (*48*). Roman troops slaughter the barbarian men. One soldier is depicted about to bring his sword down onto the bare back of a partially stunned male barbarian, who crouches on the ground on all fours. Another Roman soldier grabs a woman by the hair as she attempts to flee the village with her child. Her garment has fallen away from her right shoulder to expose her bare breast, a depiction that may itself be laden with symbolism and which appears to be another attempt by the artist responsible to somehow eroticise the violent conduct of the Roman troops in their dealings with the barbarian women. The woman holds out her arms as if in mute defence, but otherwise her posture suggests that she is resigned to her fate. A slaughtered barbarian man lies dead on the ground behind the woman and it could be assumed that he was her husband and the child's father. If so, this image of a family split asunder by reason of their resistance to the mighty power of Rome was deployed here quite cynically and in a context where there is no pendant motif celebrating the security and happiness of the Roman family, as can be seen in other, earlier examples of state art.

That there is always sexual tension and sexual violence between the men of an invading or victorious force and the women of a conquered area is unfortunately and sadly true for all conflicts, ancient and modern. While the hair-pulling scenes on the *Gemma Augustea* and the Column of Marcus Aurelius are isolated examples in Roman art, they may have derived from the hair-pulling motif in a mythological battle on the Altar of Zeus at Pergamon[15] and could thus be construed as being stock Graeco-Roman images. Nevertheless, they were used in contexts which, in the case of the Augustan example, denoted a generalised state of mistreatment of a captive and, in that of the Antonine image, a more

48 The sacking of a German village and violence against a barbarian woman. Scene xx. The Column of Marcus Aurelius, Rome. (Photo: Graham Norrie, after Petersen *et al.* 1896)

focused use in the context of the fate of female victims in the German campaigns of the time. The Aphrodisias Julio-Claudian depiction of Claudius physically overcoming and conquering *Britannia* is an altogether different kind of image, but one which nonetheless denoted one version of the nature of the relationship of the male conquerors with the female conquered, between whom sexual and social boundaries were perhaps deemed not to exist.

In Scene CIV (*49*) a group of women prisoners and their children is herded together in the background of the scene, one of the women cradling an infant in her arms, another holding onto her small child's hand as he or she is touched sympathetically by one of the other women. In the foreground, a Roman soldier is depicted pushing an evidently terrified mother and her clinging, equally frightened, son towards the main group of prisoners. Her escape is blocked by the upheld shield of a second soldier. The mother protectively encircles her son with one arm, while she holds the other arm up in a defensive gesture. A third soldier,

49 Barbarian women prisoners. Scene CIV. The Column of Marcus Aurelius, Rome. (Photo: Graham Norrie, after Petersen *et al.* 1896)

again in the foreground, is shown dragging a young, childless woman away from the group. He pulls her by the left arm, while she holds up her right arm in evident protest. The nature of her imminent fate is uncertain, as is also the case in other similar scenes of women and children being pushed forward by Roman troops.

Another scene that has elicited great debate (Scene LXIX) involves a Roman soldier walking behind a row of four women prisoners in the background of the scene, accompanied by two small children (*50*). Male barbarian prisoners are being herded along by another Roman soldier in the foreground. The Roman soldier with the women is carrying a shield in his left hand and in his right hand he is holding a barbarian baby, presumably the child of the woman in front of him whose attention appears to be on the walking small child with her. Is the soldier helping the woman by carrying her baby while she attends to her other, older frightened child or has he, in fact, just snatched this infant out of her arms for some reason? One interpretation would elicit sympathy from us, the other horror. There can be no definitive answer to this question and the interpretation

50 Barbarian women prisoners. Petersen's 'joke' scene occurs in the background. Scene LXIX. The Column of Marcus Aurelius, Rome. (Photo: Graham Norrie, after Petersen *et al.* 1896)

must remain open. However, Eugen Petersen, the man responsible for the publication of the first full photographic record of the column frieze, thought that this might have been intended to somehow be a humorous scene, that some sort of joke was intended here involving the soldier playing with the baby in a friendly way.[16] The finding of this unlikely joke has surprisingly itself elicited some singularly unamusing comment, along with the equally plausible suggestion that we might interpret the Roman soldier as trying to hand the child back to its mother.[17] A sympathetic gesture in that case once more.

Along with the processional lines of female captives being guarded by Roman troops already described, there are a number of other types of scenes of women captives. In one instance a large group of women captives is being led away into exile, along with captured flocks of animals (Scene LXXIII) (*51*). One woman grasps the arm of another, in an apparently comforting gesture, while a third woman turns her worried face towards the woman behind her, as if seeking reassurance. Women prisoners are also shown in some distress in Scene LXXXV (*52*), waiting for a group of Roman soldiers to cross over a pontoon-bridge, presumably before they are led over themselves. One soldier, having just crossed the bridge, bundles a woman and child ahead of him or out of his way; she turns her head around towards him, frightened and uncertain. In another scene (Scene XVII) showing one of the largest groups of prisoners on the column, men, women and children huddle close together in the foreground while in the background can be seen Marcus Aurelius himself with some of his staff officers (*53*). The appearance of these captives before Marcus unites the themes of the victory of the good soldier-emperor and the comprehensive defeat of the barbarian peoples that play out around the whole column. One can only guess at the eventual fate of these groups of women captives, but in portraying groups of exclusively female barbarians in these instances a very specific point was being made about the gendered nature of conquest and Roman imperialism. In another image (Scene LXXXV) (*54*), two probably highly important women prisoners are shown being transported away in a heavily guarded bullock cart from a Roman camp where they have been temporarily incarcerated.

Taken together, these scenes seem to be suggesting that war is inevitably something that affects all society, and that women and men are equally affected, even if as victims rather than active protagonists. It is unfortunately the case that the objectifying process of war has a numbing effect on the maintenance of sexual codes and barriers, and that the breaking down of these vital social constructions, or their deliberate suspension as a policy of conquest or war, leads to the kind of violence against women in war so blatantly shown on parts of the column. Portrayal of such events without the masking and filtering gauze of allegory or allusion was something quite new and revealing in Roman art. A comparison with the scenes involving women on Trajan's Column is instructive. There, barbarian women were captured or taken as hostages. They were present at scenes of siege and to the rear of battle, but nowhere were they shown being mistreated or killed as part of the general routine of war, as seems to be the message on the Aurelian Column. The only jarring scene involving women on Trajan's Column was one showing Dacian women torturing captured Roman soldiers, a scene so extraordinary in that context that it can be interpreted as probably relating to a recorded, notorious incident from the Dacian wars or as an allusion to the inherent cruelty of Dacian and barbarian women in general.[18]

The column frieze does not, of course, simply portray Roman violence against barbarian women. As will be discussed in Chapter Seven the column is, in fact, infamous for portraying images of violence in warfare in general, principally against the male barbarian opponents of Rome in these wars. Beheadings, executions and spearings of male enemies are depicted quite explicitly. Dead or mutilated bodies are routinely pictured, as indeed are dead animals. The barbarian women and children depicted, however, are not active participants in

51 Barbarian women prisoners. Scene LXXIII. The Column of Marcus Aurelius, Rome. (Photo: Graham Norrie, after Petersen *et al.* 1896)

52 Barbarian women prisoners. Scene LXXXV. The Column of Marcus Aurelius, Rome. (Photo: Graham Norrie, after Petersen *et al.* 1896)

53 Mass surrender of barbarians, including women and children. Scene XVII. The Column of Marcus Aurelius, Rome. (Photo: Graham Norrie, after Petersen *et al.* 1896).

54 Two élite
barbarian
women prisoners
are escorted
away in a wagon.
Scene LXXXV.
The Column of
Marcus Aurelius,
Rome. (Photo:
Graham Norrie,
after Petersen *et
al.* 1896)

the war, they are civilians. Their role is almost completely passive, and when
resistance of any kind on their part is portrayed, it is shown to be futile
It is the grinding inevitability of their fate – rape, death or slavery – that
underpins their depiction.

How can these images be read, bearing in mind that the way that we can
read the column today with the aid of a photographic record in front of us is
completely different from the way in which the ancient viewer might have read
the column, leaving aside the issue of the gender, status and ethnicity of our
notional viewer? They might have been guided by the programmatic prompts,
they might not have. They might have been able to see or have noticed scenes
of violence against women, they might not have. They might have viewed these
scenes as being part and parcel of an honest depiction of warfare, they might
not have. They might have viewed these scenes as being unusual, they might
not have. Viewing of these scenes might have triggered a sympathetic response
from the viewer, they might not have. Viewing of these scenes might have

triggered revulsion in the viewer, they might not have and most probably did not. And so on. In other words, we cannot ever hope to recreate a contemporary viewer's response to the column, nor can we divorce our own viewing from our technological advantage in viewing and our western cultural milieu in which violence against women is condemned as a matter of course, although in some respects it is still a taboo issue.

It has been commented on that many of the barbarian women on the column frieze are highly expressive in their gestures towards one another and, of course, towards their children when these are portrayed.[19] Some of the women captives herded together by Roman troops reach out and touch other women in a reassuring gesture of solidarity. Were these expressive gestures of solidarity intended to be viewed sympathetically by the Roman viewer and to balance in their mind the images of violence against women? Again, this is another issue which must be considered when discussing these female images.

The scenes of violence against women do not represent the portrayal of soldiers somehow out of control, of the breakdown of military discipline; they represent perhaps the first portrayal on a Roman imperial monument of what some have called the collateral damage of war, a more honest portrayal of the carnage and randomness of war that did not enter the, in comparison, somewhat anodyne pictorial representation of war on Trajan's Column.[20] But why there was a change in the policy of what was to be portrayed as an acceptable part of the conduct of war is less easy to discern. Indeed, was it really a change of policy and not simply a return to some earlier modes of the portrayal of Roman conquest by the use of the metaphor of sexual conquest? Several eroticised images of the conquest of barbarian lands personified as female figures date from the time of the Julio-Claudian emperors, as was noted above, and highlight perhaps a further model for the smaller-scale scenes of conquest by individual soldiers on the Aurelian column, that 'the masculine sexual conquest of feminized space … had a very real, non-metaphorical dimension'.[21]

In Cassius Dio's account of events around AD 166, when a large force of Germans 'from across the Rhine, advanced as far as Italy and inflicted many injuries upon the Romans', he goes on to recount how these invaders were repulsed by Marcus. Curiously, Dio reports that 'among the corpses of the barbarians there were found even women's bodies in armour', an occurrence remarkable enough to merit mention here, even if this was really based on a battlefield rumour rather than on a properly attested instance of this.[22] It does perhaps suggest that knowledge of a true or rumoured event like this might have circulated in the Roman army for some time afterwards and that in Marcus's later wars against the Germans some Roman soldiers may have consequently viewed German women as potential combatants rather than innocent bystanders. Stories such as this have often been cited as motives behind the rationalising of more recent instances of ethnic cleansing, where women and children were as much the targets of violence as were male combatants.

As to the scenes involving children, their presence is once more a way for the programme of the column to be used to demonstrate to the Roman viewer the depth of the defeat of these barbarian peoples, that such a defeat would resonate for several generations and that victory in these wars was not just a quick-fix solution to problems on the frontiers of the empire.[23] These children are witnesses to many physically violent acts on the column and some suffer physical violence themselves. Others are separated from their parents or their mothers, an act of psychological violence that may mark the start of a lifetime of dislocation if sold into slavery; dislocation from one's biological parents, dislocation from one's extended family, dislocation from one's tribe, dislocation from one's tribal culture and ethnic material culture, dislocation from one's house or home, dislocation from one's homeland and natural environment, dislocation from one's former status and possibly even from one's name, and dislocation from one's destined future.

The male gaze

There were undoubtedly significant variations in the uses and meanings of the image of the male barbarian and of the female barbarian in Roman art, and to perhaps a lesser extent, of the barbarian child. There may also have been some significance not only in the number of instances in which barbarian women appeared in Roman art, but also in the matter of whether they appeared on their own, as mothers accompanied by young children, with a male companion or husband, or with a male companion and children as an emblematic family unit. The female barbarian was the most common mortal woman, as opposed to goddesses or personifications, in Roman imperial art. This must have reflected not only a distinct historical role for the female barbarian in the visual narrative of Roman history, but also a very distinct perception of her in the minds of the viewers of these artworks.[24]

The image of the female captive, either represented explicitly by the image of a barbarian woman and her fate, or implicitly by the use of female personifications in a way that was at odds with the original Greek conception of such figures, is a tellingly common motif. Its use related to the gendered nature of Roman imperial power, and almost certainly also testified to a fear of female transgression and unsuitable behaviour, both by barbarian women and by the women of Rome and the empire.

Part of a strategy of defining acceptable female roles and behaviour included the employment of mythological exemplars in Roman art for didactic purposes. Under Augustus, for example, the appearance of depictions of the Rape of the Sabine Women and the Punishment of Tarpeia in the Basilica Aemilia would have sent a very clear message to its viewers about Roman and non-Roman relationships and about male-female relationships in Augustan Rome (55).[25] Again, the sculptural frieze of Domitian's Forum, the so-called *Forum Transitorium* in

55 The punishment of Tarpeia. Part of the frieze from the Basilica Aemilia. Museo Palazzo
Massimo alle Terme, Rome. (Photo: Author)

Rome, concerned itself with mythological imagery used in an imperial context,
images that were almost exclusively of women, something that was itself unusual.
Here, encapsulated within images of the act of weaving, were ideas relating to
the value and dignity of female creative pursuits – in this context a dignity and
moral value defined and assigned by male imperial ideology – while Arachne was
present as a warning of the potential fate of those women who transgressed.[26]
These were messages to the women of Rome.

Some years ago Barbara Kellum published an interesting paper called *The Phallus
as Signifier: The Forum of Augustus and Rituals of Masculinity*[27] which is of relevance
here to the discussion of gendered messages encoded in the art and architecture of
Rome. Kellum here described Augustus's Forum as 'a sexually charged, gendered
masculine environment'[28] and discussed whether the groundplan of the forum
was in fact deliberately intended to be phallic in shape as part of the overall
scheme to celebrate Roman masculinity here. Such an analysis could indeed have
been usefully extended to the phallic-like obelisk that formed the pointer of
the *Horologium Augusti*, the Augustan Sundial in the *Campus Martius* that is now
re-erected in Piazza del Parlamento. With the erection of the Column of Marcus
Aurelius in *c*.AD 192 the *Campus Martius* would then have been graced with four
such thrusting phallic monuments – the Augustan obelisk, Trajan's Column,
the Column of Antoninus Pius and Marcus's column – that perhaps together
served to emphasise the potency of Roman imperial masculinity. Perhaps in such
an environment the use of images of an eroticised Victory and eroticised, but
suffering, barbarian women on Marcus's column is more understandable.

The Roman use of ethnic personifications, an artistic strategy adopted from
Greek art, could be both positive and negative in intent and usage. However, it did

not require a great deal of imagination to understand the implications inherent in the regular equation of a woman's body with conquered or subject territory, and it did not necessarily require that this equation be made overly explicit, as in the case of the Claudius/*Britannia* and Nero/*Armenia* sculptures from the *Sebasteion* at Aphrodisias.

In the earlier Roman empire, before what could be called the Aurelian watershed, that time around which attitudes to barbarian peoples seem to have hardened, there may have been more of an emphasis, in terms of numbers of appearances, on the use of more mixed-gender images of barbarian groups and peoples. It can be suggested that, in some depictions of barbarian couples, the fact that the man was bound or in chains, and that the woman remained untied, in a mournful or dejected pose, indicated a definite strategy of suggesting barbarian male aggression and female passivity, for the woman evidently posed no threat and was therefore not constrained. All the more extraordinary, then, was the depiction of the Dacian women torturing Roman prisoners on Trajan's Column.

When barbarian couples were depicted, this would seem to have been a way of staking out some element of common ground, of a common humanity between the Romans and the barbarian peoples portrayed. An absence of such pairings could be construed as the opposite – a declaration of a state of complete otherness. As well as sharing common humanity with the Roman couple, the barbarian couple, though defeated and often shown dejected and distraught, could then be transformed by the incorporation of their land into the empire and subject territory of Rome. While they, themselves, may not have become citizens, their children and their children's children may have achieved such a status, perhaps through the service of a son in the auxiliary units of the Roman army. A people defeated by Rome was not necessarily a despised people. However, the wars fought by Marcus were not wars of incorporation as such, though he may have hoped to eventually create new provinces in captured lands, and therefore it is this spirit of civilising *Romanitas* that is missing from the depictions of warfare and of violence against barbarian women on Marcus's column.

Hate and War

The reign of Marcus's predecessor, Antoninus Pius, was on the whole an era of peace and great prosperity for Rome. Antoninus Pius was judged to have been one of the four good emperors up to this time. However, Marcus Aurelius and Lucius Verus, the adopted heirs of the Antonine Dynasty, were to reign over what was then an almost unprecedented era of uprisings and major wars against the Parthians in the east and the *Marcomanni* in Germany between AD 161 and 180, when Marcus died on campaign with the army. This period also saw a fundamental change in the way in which art was used to express imperial necessity and deep political uncertainty. Maybe this was reflected in the scenes of warfare and violence on the Column of Marcus Aurelius which form the subject of this chapter. It was also probably reflected in a significant, but temporary, move away from imperial exclusivity in the use of images of victory, towards a situation in which senior military men of the era celebrated their achievements through the commissioning of what are now known as battle sarcophagi, which will also be discussed here. Perhaps there had always been a strain of violent imagery in military art, particularly in the Roman provinces where more simple and direct images might have employed to put across messages to viewers about the victorious nature of Roman imperialism.

Atrocity exhibition

Almost entirely absent from the relief narratives on the Aurelian Column are the types of camp and fortification construction scenes and endless scenes of the army on the march that played such a large and significant part in the artistic scheme of Trajan's Column, as was discussed in Chapter Two. Roman victory on the later column perhaps needed depicting in a different way, with less obvious exertion on the part of the army and more in the way of a clinical approach to warfare and Roman dealings with their enemies. It is, therefore, analysis of the many battle scenes that must lead any reading of the Column of Marcus Aurelius, these scenes probably making up just under half of the scenes on the column,[1] though, as has been stressed throughout this book, the column cannot, and should not, be read as a literal, chronological commentary on the Marcomannic wars.

In these battle scenes there is often almost a sense of panic and frantic endeavour on the part of the Roman forces that seems to be at odds with the clinical order of many of the military manoeuvres depicted on Trajan's Column. While the composition and style of the Trajanic column's battles suggested a sense of order, stressed by the general uniformity of many of the figures of massed troops, on the Aurelian column disharmonic forms, awkward figural poses, and jagged composition together created almost the opposite effect (56). It has even been argued that there is not simply just a gestural difference between the images of Romans and barbarians on the column, but also that the presentation of their faces differs; the Romans' faces 'are either juvenile and smooth, or rather uncouth … [representing] … military virtues such as energy, resoluteness and efficiency', whereas the barbarians' faces are 'characterised as evil or – more commonly – are shown in a state of pain, fear or terror'.[2]

A programmatic analysis of the battle scenes on the column has been undertaken by Felix Pirson[3] who calculated that of the one hundred and sixteen individual scenes on the column as defined by Eugen Petersen thirty-six 'are apportioned to battles or fights and eleven to violence related to war'.[4] Around four hundred and

56 Battle scene and pile of barbarian bodies. Scene LXXXIX. The Column of Marcus Aurelius, Rome. (Photo: Graham Norrie, after Petersen *et al.* 1896)

seventy individual figures appear in the battle scenes, of whom two hundred and ninety-five are shown 'in the context of fighting'.[5] Of these, one hundred and sixty-six are Romans and one hundred and twenty-two are barbarians, perhaps indicating that an impression of Roman superiority in the wars could be seen from this numerical superiority of images on the column, though this is unlikely due to problems of visibility. An analysis of the types of depictions as represented by their stances indicated that repetition of a relatively small number of types probably enhanced visibility. In general, Roman stance types were active – that is involving the figures in attack – while most barbarian stances were passive – that is involving the figures in defence or being injured, dead or dying (57).[6]

The barbarian stance types included many awkward poses whose disharmonic nature, emphasised by repetition, contrasted with the less awkward, more harmonic poses of the Roman figures, again this sense of order being emphasised by repetition. To the viewer this general contrast may have been readily apparent and indicative of the difference between Roman and barbarian, between victor and vanquished and between civilisation and barbarity.

57 Battle scene. Scene XXVIII. The Column of Marcus Aurelius, Rome. (Photo: Graham Norrie, after Petersen *et al.* 1896)

Pirson calculated that only about a third of the barbarians in battle scenes could strictly be defined as fighting, as opposed to 'falling from horseback', 'cowering' (*58*), being 'dead or dying' and 'panicking and fleeing' (*59*).[7] Indeed, the very one-sided nature of the battle scenes has occasioned comment from a number of authorities and that 'Roman victory does not appear as the result of a struggle with a worthy and brave antagonist; but, rather, that the barbarians are shown either taking cover or begging for mercy'.[8] It is difficult to accept this interpretation as strictly true, when it is considered that two of the more iconic scenes on the column involve the Germans laying siege to a Roman camp with a highly sophisticated siege tower (Scene XI), requiring the intervention of the Miracle of the Thunderbolt to halt the siege in dramatic fashion, and a pendant siege scene where the Germans are fiercely fighting against Roman troops formed up into a *testudo* formation (Scene LIV). Rather than running away or hiding, the barbarians are expending considerable energy in an attempt to repel the Roman assault, with numerous missiles raining down onto the massed Roman shields.

A number of individual scenes of battle and warfare will now be discussed as examples of the way in which violence underpinned the overall message of

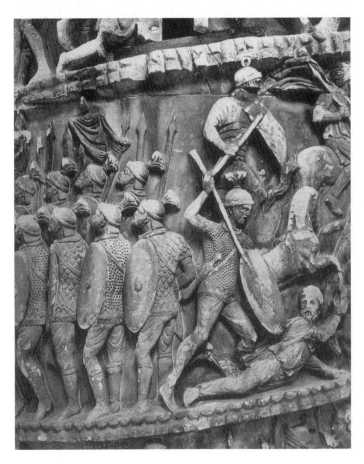

58 Spearing of a prostrate barbarian man. Scene XCVI. The Column of Marcus Aurelius, Rome. (Photo: Graham Norrie, after Petersen *et al.* 1896)

59 Battle scene. Scene
XCVII. The Column of
Marcus Aurelius, Rome.
(Photo: Graham Norrie,
after Petersen *et al.* 1896)

the column frieze as it might have been transmitted to a contemporary viewer.
Roman violence against barbarian women has been considered in detail as a
separate issue in Chapter Six.

The Roman forces have no sooner crossed the Danube at the start of the first
war (Scene III) (*60*) than they are depicted in the act of destroying an abandoned
German village (Scene VII), the torching and clearance of native villages
being repeated elsewhere on the column, for example in Scene XX (*61*), as if
to emphasise the nature of the warfare being conducted by the Roman forces.
Soldiers then bring before the emperor two mounted barbarian male captives
who had evidently not been able to flee the environs of the sleighted village in
good time (Scene VIII). Two dead barbarians, perhaps executed prisoners, whose
inert bodies sprawl one on top of the other, appear in the foreground of the scene.
In the background, a Roman soldier pushes his shield into the back of another
semi-naked barbarian prisoner, the posture of the Roman suggesting that he may
be about to kill the prisoner with his sword. The barbarian, his bare back to the
viewer, reaches up one arm, perhaps in a gesture of pain or despair, and almost
appears to brace himself against the frame of the relief space. Thus, early in the

frieze, at perhaps a low enough level for contemporary viewers to have made out these scenes, images of a Roman scorched-earth policy in operation have been presented to the viewer, along with a similarly clinical attitude to the barbarian defeated being shown by the images of the captives juxtaposed with the dead bodies and the possible execution scene. Numerous other scenes of captives being taken appear on the column (*e.g. 62*).

While in Chapter Four an extended discussion of the depiction of the two Weather Miracles on the column was presented, it is worth returning to the scene of the Miracle of the Rains (Scene XVI) to once more highlight the shocking portrayal there of a vast heap of barbarian corpses, weaponry and a slaughtered horse. This motif, a pile of bodies, also recurs during the depiction of the second campaign (Scene CIX) (*63*).

The brutal treatment and routine execution of prisoners is starkly portrayed in a number of places on the column, but most tellingly by a scene of execution

60 The Roman troops cross the Danube bridge. Scene III. The Column of Marcus Aurelius, Rome. (Photo: Graham Norrie, after Petersen *et al.* 1896).

61 The sacking of a German village. Scene xx. The Column of Marcus Aurelius, Rome. (Photo: Graham Norrie, after Petersen *et al.* 1896)

62 Barbarian male prisoners. Scene LXXVII. The Column of Marcus Aurelius, Rome. (Photo: Graham Norrie, after Petersen *et al.* 1896)

63 A frantic battle and a pile of barbarian bodies. Scene CIX. The Column of Marcus Aurelius, Rome. (Photo: Graham Norrie, after Petersen *et al.* 1896)

(Scene LXI), where the beheading of barbarian male prisoners is overseen by Roman troops, while the actual act of holding the bound male captives and striking the blow is carried out by their compatriots (*64*). It is not entirely clear whether they are being forced to do this, or whether these are barbarian mercenaries whose complicity has been bought by Rome. The bound prisoners, their faces in some cases contorted with terror, stand in line awaiting their fate, while crumpled bodies lie nearby, their severed heads resting on the ground beside.

Another Antonine beheading scene, though less detailed in its composition, can be found on the largest and most elaborate of the legionary distance slabs from the Antonine Wall in Scotland. The Bridgeness slab [9] consists of a central panel bearing an inscription citing its dedicators as the *Legio* II Augusta, flanked by two sculptured scenes, the one on the right portraying a Roman cavalryman and four barbarian figures and the one on the left being a scene of religious sacrifice

64 Mass executions. Scene LXI. The Column of Marcus Aurelius, Rome. (Photo: Graham Norrie, after Petersen *et al.* 1896)

65 The Bridgeness legionary distance slab. (Photo: copyright National Museums of Scotland, Edinburgh)

following Roman victory (65). In the right hand scene the Roman cavalryman rides at a gallop, with a spear raised in his right hand, while in the foreground of the scene are the barbarian men in various poses, one seemingly ridden down by the charging horseman, a second falling to the ground with a broken-off spear shaft sticking out of his back, a third seated on the ground to the left. He looks away from the field of battle and gazes towards the viewer, while the fourth figure, a headless, evidently bound, torso, sits to the right, his severed head lying on the ground next to his body.

Rather than this being a representation of a single cavalryman attacking four enemies, it is argued here that it may, in fact, be recording the fate of a single barbarian man who appears four times, the first time being overcome by the

Roman cavalryman and in his fourth and final appearance being shown as an executed prisoner.[10] The battle scene here quite obviously owed its inspiration to the horseman-and-fallen-enemy type of auxiliary cavalry tombstone of the first and second centuries which is discussed further below.

The severed head of a barbarian is presented to the emperor some time later on the column (Scene LXVI), this kind of grotesque trophy being familiar from its occurrence also on Trajan's Column. At the emperor's feet stands a number of other Roman soldiers with a live barbarian captive, though his immediate guard holds him by the hair in a violent mimicry of the head held above. A few scenes later there occurs another horrific scene of execution (Scene LXVIII). A group of six Roman foot soldiers, with shields held in one hand and lances in the other, is caught in the act of spearing and killing a number of unarmed barbarian men. One barbarian already lies dead on the ground and another, as a spear is thrust deep into his shoulder, lets out a scream of agony that is captured on his face by the artist in a pornography of violence. Being herded towards this killing field (Scene LXIX) are four more male prisoners and a number of barbarian women, two of them holding babies and another touching her young son or daughter who nestles up close to her body. This woman holds one arm protectively across her breast. Whether these men and women are being brought to watch the executions taking place in the adjacent scene or whether they are being led to their own deaths is unclear. An analysis of this iconic image of the screaming barbarian man and of its reception forms the basis of Chapter Five.

One of the most shocking scenes on the whole column (Scene XX) is the sacking of a German village, with the emperor and his attendant officers being shown as spectators at the event. Roman troops slaughter the barbarian men. One soldier is depicted about to bring his sword down onto a barbarian man already partially stunned and on the ground on all fours, with his bare back to the looming figure of the Roman trooper. Another Roman soldier grabs a woman by the hair as she attempts to flee the village with her child. Her garment has fallen away from her right shoulder to expose her bare breast, a depiction that may itself be laden with symbolism. A slaughtered barbarian man lies dead on the ground behind the woman and it could be assumed that he was her husband and the child's father.

Numerous other scenes of frenzied battle appear on the column; four further representative examples are reproduced here to illustrate the unrelenting ferocity of the wars, including a battle near a barbarian stronghold that is turning into a massacre and rout (Scene XX) (*66*), a bloody engagement in progress as Roman reinforcements arrive by boat (Scene XXXIV) (*67*) and two depictions of the spearing of falling or fallen barbarian men (Scenes LXIII and LXVII) (*68 & 69*).

The final, upper reliefs on the Column of Marcus Aurelius portray barbarian peoples going off into exile with their belongings and their animals. Most are on foot, some on horseback, a few ride in bullock carts. The exiles include both men and women, but no children are depicted, which may be of significance. Such

66 Battle outside a barbarian stronghold. Scene xx. The Column of Marcus Aurelius, Rome. (Photo: Graham Norrie, after Petersen *et al.* 1896)

67 Battle scene, with Roman soldiers crossing a river in boats. Scene xxxiv. The Column of Marcus Aurelius, Rome. (Photo: Graham Norrie, after Petersen *et al.* 1896)

68 Spearing of a barbarian man. Scene LXIII. The Column of Marcus Aurelius, Rome. (Photo: Graham Norrie, after Petersen *et al.* 1896)

69 Spearing of a barbarian man. Scene LXVII. The Column of Marcus Aurelius, Rome. (Photo: Graham Norrie, after Petersen *et al.* 1896)

a scene of the defeated, impotent enemy leaving the arena of combat is quite a traditional trope in the context of Roman imperial art, and brings to mind, in particular, similar scenes on the *Tropaeum Traiani* at Adamklissi.

This brief, selective discussion of the battle scenes on the Column of Marcus Aurelius may appear to be biased towards the discussion of cruelty and death. However, this nevertheless represents a true reflection of the overall iconography of the monument. It was not, of course, intended to be a victory monument or a war memorial, though its decorative scheme may have suggested otherwise, but while such monuments concentrating on war alone had been set up in the provinces, for example at Orange in *Gallia Narbobensis* and at Adamklissi in Upper Moesia, the appearance here in Rome of such an structure as a funerary monument was unprecedented.[11] It might perhaps have been expected that a Roman monument would endeavour to convey other more subtle and complex messages relating to imperial policies or aspirations in the way that this had been achieved by Trajan's Column. But on the Aurelian column, the barbarian had simply become a dehumanised body, as has been noted elsewhere in this book, a bloodied victim whose defeat at the hands of Rome was inevitable and whose selling into slavery would debase him further, if he had not already ended his days in a stinking heap of rotting bodies, food for the carrion birds and on display for the edification of the Roman viewer.

A shying-away from engagement with the bloodiness and gore of the column's content, or attempting to view its frieze as debased, not to say almost degenerate, classical art, sullied by the acceptance of trends of portrayal prevalent in military, plebeian and provincial art of an earlier period, would represent a failure to come to terms with the reality of the political situation and the imperial psyche at this time. The violent images on the Column of Marcus Aurelius need to be understood not only in the context of the overall programme of decoration on the column, but also to be seen in the context of all violent images of the time and particularly in the context of images on Antonine battle sarcophagi and in military art. In Chapter Five it has been argued that the violent images on the column need to be viewed within the even broader context of the regular, institutionalised manifestation of violence in certain areas of Roman society, including the games and violent judicial punishment. Only then can we really hope to start to understand the use of such images that so jar with and offend modern sensibilities.

Dead souls

If the highly violent scenes of combat and warfare on the Column of Marcus Aurelius are going to be understood fully then, as noted above, they need to be viewed in a broader artistic and cultural context. Of particular interest, therefore, is a highly distinctive group of about twenty or so decorated battle sarcophagi dating from the mid- to later second century AD, on which similar, dense and violent scenes of Roman-barbarian warfare appeared.[12] As with any such assemblage of objects, many of the sarcophagi are not precisely dated and there are a number of chronological outliers to the main group, of which the best example is the later Ludovisi sarcophagus which will be omitted from the discussion here, though it should be seen as part of the same artistic phenomenon.[13] These sarcophagi represent unusual examples of the widespread use in Roman aristocratic circles of what had generally become imperial artistic motifs and tropes in a non-imperial, private context. Perhaps imperial and aristocratic concerns about political instability and compromised security on the frontiers of the empire merged at this time in a way that had not previously occurred.

However, it should also be noted that other types of decorated sarcophagi were equally, if not more, common in this period, including so-called biographical sarcophagi and sarcophagi bearing mythological decoration, which again were often decorated with images alluding to Roman military victory, such allusive strategies being very much in keeping with the legacy of Hellenistic art. Battles between Greeks and Amazons and the Indian Victory of Bacchus were perhaps the most obvious conveyors of allusions to the virtue of the dead man being commemorated, and to real struggle and real heroism in contemporary warfare. In a more abstract way, perhaps, virtue of this kind could also be celebrated by the illustration of the punishment of vice on *sarcophagi*, a phenomenon that began earlier than Marcus's reign, but which in its continuation throughout his reign very much reflected the emperor's particular concern with virtue. Scenes of this kind included the gods punishing the giants, the slaughter of the Niobids, or the goddess Diana bringing about the death of Actaeon by his own hunting hounds. Hunting sarcophagi, very much a Hadrianic phenomenon, were also popular in the Antonine period, the hunt again being allusive and acting as a metaphor for heroic achievement in general.

Three individual sarcophagi will be discussed in detail here in chronological order, starting with the *Via Appia* sarcophagus of *c.*AD 150, followed by the so-called *Clementia* sarcophagus of *c.*AD 170 and the Portonaccio sarcophagus of *c.*AD 180–190.

The front panel of a sarcophagus from a site on the *Via Appia* in Rome was decorated with a battle between Romans and Gauls.[14] By the mid-second century, the Gauls were very much historic enemies of Rome and not a contemporary threat and it must therefore be assumed that the decorative scheme was deliberately anachronistic in both its choice of protagonists for what was intended to be a symbolic battle, and in its style and composition which harked back to Hellenistic models, particularly the so-called Attalid Gauls. Some of the poses of the barbarians – one supporting himself with outstretched arm on the ground and another holding off a Roman soldier who grips him by the hair – were stock motifs from the long Graeco-Roman tradition of battle pictures. In contrast, in the narrow register of decoration on the sarcophagus lid is depicted a line of seated, defeated and despondent barbarian captives, with captured arms and armour filling in the background, in echo of the trophies which flank the battle scene below. The three male captives depicted here are all bound, and of the three barbarian women, one holds up her hand to her head in pain or anguish, while the other two are shown with children, one child comforting its huddled and brooding mother and the other child being held protectively by its mother. Both the action of the defeat of the barbarians, and the consequences of that defeat, are juxtaposed to quite dramatic effect.

The *Clementia* sarcophagus in the Vatican Museums[15] is decorated, as the coffin's modern name implies, with a scene in which a bearded Roman military commander gives audience to a large group of heavily guarded barbarian men, women and children seeking clemency. One of the barbarian men goes down on his knees before the victorious general, while the other two remain standing. They all have expressions of pain or anguish on their faces, but particularly striking, and surprisingly poignant in the context of the art of the period, is a kneeling woman and her small child, who rubs at his eye with one hand while touching his mother's arm with the other. The woman reaches out her arm to comfort the crying child. At the same time as giving the barbarians an audience, the general is being crowned by Victory. The scene is flanked at each end of the sarcophagus panel by figures of bound male barbarian captives sitting beneath a trophy, each of these figures looking up, with their heads turned away from the central scene.

On the short sides of the sarcophagus are further barbarians. On one side, a wagon is depicted carrying prisoners, perhaps being paraded in a triumphal procession in Rome. The prisoners consist of a woman and her child, perhaps in echo of the two figures on the front of the sarcophagus, the woman seated facing towards the back of the cart, with her head in her hands in the mourning-captive pose, while the unattended child rests one arm across his mother's shoulder and with his other reaches out to, and touches, the spear held by the Roman soldier who accompanies the cart. This mixture of a sorrowful scene tempered by the joking playfulness of the small child is unusual. On the other short side of the sarcophagus are seated captives guarded by Roman troops. Two women and a man appear here, one of the women again depicted in a huddled, mourning-captive pose.

Perhaps the best known battle sarcophagus is the Portonaccio sarcophagus, of a late-Antonine date, perhaps commissioned by Aulus Iulius Pompilius, a general under Marcus Aurelius (*70*).[16] This consists of the main body of the sarcophagus, which is carved on three sides only, and a flat, decorated lid. The main scene on the front panel is a complex and frenzied battle scene, involving Roman forces and Germanic barbarians. The sheer density of the composition, with fighting troops almost intertwined one with another, is quite striking and claustrophobic. The seething mass of interlocked bodies produces an almost decorative effect when viewed from a distance.

The principal figure on the front of the sarcophagus is a Roman cavalryman at the centre of a squadron of riders who are battling fiercely with the

70 The Portonaccio sarcophagus; Museo Nazionale delle Terme, Rome. (Photo DAIR 61.1399)

barbarian footsoldiers all around them. Other Roman infantrymen take part in hand-to-hand combat, principally towards the bottom third of the sarcophagus. Barbarian bodies fall to the ground or are contorted into awkward shapes as they lie there in their death throes, many trampled under horses' hooves in the heat and confusion of battle. The faces of the barbarian protagonists variously display looks of pain or of horror, while the faces of the Roman soldiers remain largely impassive. Roman soldiers spear the enemy, stab or hack at them with their swords in a seeming frenzy. This desperate battle scene is flanked by two trophies, beneath each of which stands a pair of barbarians, one male and one female in each case. They are not bound, but their distress in defeat is evident.

On the two short sides of the sarcophagus are scenes of barbarian prisoners being led across a pontoon bridge and another of barbarians surrendering. On the sarcophagus lid are various scenes of both public and military life and of the deceased's private life. The lid is book-ended by two large masks. Looking from right to left are represented first what appears to be a scene of the bathing of a child, a marriage being celebrated in the central scene, while the final scene shows barbarians begging for mercy from a seated Roman general. Behind the general's stool, a Roman soldier stands guard over barbarian prisoners huddled around, and sat beneath, a trophy. A dejected-looking barbarian mother and her child are at the forefront of the group of captives, in quite evident contrast to the young Roman woman and her child at the other end of the lid. These three scenes can be considered to be obliquely biographical, in that they do not necessarily directly relate to the life of the deceased, rather they refer to qualities and virtues that would have been, at least in theory, personified in the actions and life of the dead man.

A brief comparison of the front panels of the three sarcophagi chosen for discussion above suggests progressive complexity in terms of numbers of figures represented in order to convey more-or-less the same basic message in each case, and probably arising from that progressive complexity in design of the front panel scene. On the *Via Appia* sarcophagus ten figures are represented, seven barbarian men and three Roman soldiers on a panel 1.25 metres in height. On the *Clementia* sarcophagus seventeen figures are depicted, comprising eight barbarian men, one barbarian woman, a barbarian child and seven Roman soldiers on a panel *c.*1.25 metres in height. On the densely-packed front panel of the Portonaccio sarcophagus thirty-three individual figures can be discerned among the twisted and interlinked mass of humanity depicted there, comprising seventeen barbarian men, two barbarian women and fourteen Roman soldiers on a panel 1.85 metres in height. Four of these figures are non-combatant barbarian prisoners, making the battle itself almost evenly matched in numerical terms.

The messages conveyed by the artworks on these three sarcophagi are then in general the same. On the *Via Appia* sarcophagus, despite the fact that the Gauls were by now a historic enemy rather than a contemporary one, this motif of a barbarian-foe-successfully-overcome may have been chosen as a reassuring reference point at a time of Roman uncertainty over the eventual outcome of their wars and battles against newer and different barbarian foes.

The overall decorative scheme of the *Clementia* sarcophagus was both traditional and at the same time novel, in that the artist introduced elements of both playfulness and pathos into the depiction of the barbarian peoples, otherwise defeated, dejected and pleading. That these elements were introduced through the medium of the image of a child, in one case to elicit sympathy and in the other to raise a smile at the child's wilfulness, rather than through that of an adult, perhaps alludes to the fact that the *clementia* of the general, and of the Roman state by association, had positively affected the future of those children and the overall future of their people or tribe. It may be that the tribe's defeat led to their incorporation within the empire and that all the benefits of *Romanitas* became theirs as a result.

Changes in attitude brought about by political crises and the perception of the breaking down of traditional roles in society were factors in the questioning of the relevance of the old perceptions of virtue. In art, these changes are best seen reflected in the decoration on the Portonaccio sarcophagus, on which small biographical scenes are relegated to the sarcophagus lid, while the sarcophagus itself is dominated by a complex and harrowing battle scene like those on the Column of Marcus Aurelius. On the sarcophagus, though, these scenes are of an entirely symbolic nature. Representations of the old virtues are nowhere to be seen, and in the battle it may be surmised that victory must be won at any cost, and that such striving is now simply an end in itself.[17]

It is hardly surprising, given the extended period of time spent by the emperor Marcus Aurelius at war and on campaign, that an over-preoccupation with military affairs and martial concerns should also have been shared by a large sector of the upper echelons of Roman society at this time. Equally that their involvement in the wars of his reign should have been commemorated in a dramatic, original way, by the commissioning of the battle sarcophagi, in a style that is both part of an overall tradition of Italian and Roman funerary art, and yet at the same time highly original in terms of its evident stylistic and narrative links with the state art that commemorated those same wars, is unusual but not surprising. Indeed, in the *Vita Marci* it is recounted how 'because in this German, or Marcomannic, war, or rather I should say in this "War of Many Nations", many nobles perished' Marcus 'erected statues in the Forum of Trajan'[18] for all of them, implying that he fully recognised the contribution being made by the Roman aristocracy to the defence of the state.

The good soldier

As Commodus was obviously intent on casting his father as a soldier-emperor on the artwork of the column, it is not altogether surprising that many of the basic themes and some stylistic traits of Roman military art were represented there alongside Roman imperial symbolism. This symbiotic relationship between the two strains of interrelated military and imperial rhetoric was also to feed into and feed off the art of the private battle sarcophagi discussed above. Indeed, it has been argued by some authorities that it was the 'debased' art of the military that had a detrimental influence and effect on the development of the state art of Late Antiquity, as if that art were not in fact an index of its own time.

The Roman army, like many such organisations, was a separate community with its own insular, institutional culture that was reflected in the art produced by, and on behalf of, the officers and soldiers serving across the empire. Almost inevitably, the image of the defeated barbarian foe was a common motif in military art, with differences in its use being dependant on the type of artefact or monument on which such images appeared, on the context of the commissioning of the art, and on regional and chronological variations.

Martial iconography was commonplace on Roman military equipment, principally on decorated breastplates, cuirasses and helmets, or on *baltei* or belts and horse armour and trappings.[19] This is something that should hardly occasion surprise, though perhaps a difference between such battle scenes in the professional milieu of the army and those deployed in the context of imperial art may be detectable. However, discussion of these items of military equipment is not strictly relevant here and attention will be concentrated instead on a small number of provincial monuments and funerary monuments which utilised images of barbarians in a way that perhaps predated the debasement of the barbarian in Roman imperial art from the time of Marcus Aurelius onwards.

Images of barbarians appear on a number of Roman legionary monuments, including a probably Domitianic arcaded monument at Mainz in Germany and the Antonine Wall legionary distance slabs from Scotland, some of which are discussed in detail elsewhere in this book. On the numerous column bases from the Mainz monument are depictions of both the Roman victors and the defeated barbarians, along with victories and trophies.[20] One of the column bases is carved with the figures of two virtually naked, barbarian men with their hands tied behind their backs and a chain running between them and fastened around their necks. Their bodies are turned round to face the viewer, their genitals fully depicted by the artist, as if to further emphasise both their vulnerability and their emasculation. They have been become less than men, impotent in their defeat. A similar message is conveyed on another of the column bases, on which a seated, weeping female barbarian is depicted. Though fully clothed, she is nevertheless a vulnerable, dejected and isolated figure here. The images of these barbarians contrast with the images of armed and determined figures of Roman legionary soldiers which also appeared on the monument.

On four of the Antonine Wall legionary distance slabs, male barbarians appear as bound captives,[21] while on the large Bridgeness stone one barbarian is shown as having been subsequently executed by beheading.[22] The captives are afforded no element of dignity, they are shown as less than men, objectified and exposed naked in their indignity in a visual narrative which objectified the barbarian men through the depiction of their dead, bound or mutilated bodies and which exiled them to a space more usually thought of as being occupied by objectified barbarian women.

In both these instances the viewer in Mainz or on the Antonine Wall in Scotland would have been left in no doubt about the nature of Roman-barbarian relationships portrayed there. Neither monument hints at pathos in their depictions of the barbarians, and Roman victory is depicted as being clinical and complete. Maybe this stark, simple message was one tailored to the demands of the celebration of Roman power in the provinces at their respective times.

Roman military funerary memorials in the provinces also sometimes used motifs of barbarian defeat to celebrate individual achievement by auxiliary soldiers, most notably the auxiliary cavalry tombstones of the first and second centuries AD found in Britain and the Rhineland, and known most commonly as *Reitertyp* tombstones.[23] There is a number of variations in the scenes on these tombstones but they generally involve a mounted cavalryman riding down a male barbarian enemy, with the final, killer blow about to be struck, or the barbarian is shown being struck, with the fallen foe either lying prostrate and looking up at the rider, or curled up in a protective huddle under the trampling hooves of the charging horse. In one instance, on a tombstone from Halton Chesters in Northumbria, the barbarian is shown trying to pull out the shaft of a spear lodged in his chest.

It is not simply that these images depict a Roman slaying a barbarian, rather we are seeing an auxiliary soldier of non-Roman origins, most of those commemorated coming from either Thracian or Gallic units, slaying a barbarian on Rome's behalf, a somewhat more complicated scenario than it might at first appear. These tombstones represented records of individual soldiers' lives and achievements both within their ethnic auxiliary units and within the Roman army as a whole. In these depictions, the fellow-cavalrymen of the deceased would have been able to recognise their own story: their ethnic or racial origins through the record of the inscription; their professional role as soldiers in the service of Rome through the wording and form of the inscription as well as more obviously through the scene depicted, and pride in their adopted personae through the detailed recreation of their arms and armour and horse trappings. Felix Pirson felt that the one-sided nature of the symbolic combat scenes on tombstones such as these and, it could be added, on other military art, particularly in the provinces, was eventually reflected in 'the appearance of symbolic poses of superiority and defeat' on the Column of Marcus Aurelius.[24]

Victory and pathos

The screaming and contorted faces of barbarians on the Column of Marcus Aurelius and on some of the Antonine battle sarcophagi and their often violent treatment at the hands of Roman troops represented a new mode of artistic depiction that went hand-in-hand with the brutal realism of the fate of these barbarian peoples.

Of course, such images could be viewed simply as examples of the realistic portrayal of the conduct and reality of war, with these barbarian victims having been as much a required part of the visual language of celebration of Roman victories as images of the victors themselves. Indeed, that was probably to a great extent true: as Mary Beard has written in relation to scenes on the Aurelian column, 'inevitably victory and pathos are two sides of the same coin; scenes of brutality are always boastful triumphalism as much as they are empathy with a suffering victim, as much displays of compassion as they are monuments of triumph'.[25] However, it is argued in this book that violent images of the barbarian opponents of Rome being humiliated in defeat on the column should be analysed not only in the specific context in which they appeared, but also more broadly in the context of changing perceptions of the nature of these enemies and the very real threat that they posed to the stability and future of the Roman empire itself.

Managing Difference

In previous chapters particular attention has been paid not only to images in which Marcus himself appears, but also to representations of the so-called Weather Miracles, of an eroticised Victory, of lurid violence against barbarian women, of frenzied battle and of the screaming barbarian man who, for some scholars, is the most iconic image on the whole column. Here attention will be focused on a miscellany of individual images, each of which in some way contributes towards an overall rhetoric about the management of difference through the programme of artworks on the column. The constructing of identities on the column is both overt and covert. The depiction of the physical appearance and clothing of the barbarian peoples represented on the column might at first glance appear to be a way of accurately representing these people. However, the general uniformity of these images of what were, in fact, many different tribal groups with their own distinct appearances and material cultures, is a reflection of a strategy to depersonalise these tribal peoples in conflict with Rome. The depiction of buildings within barbarian villages is part of a contrastive schema utilising depictions of Roman and barbarian architecture as metaphors for civilisation and barbarity, as well as for other less obvious ideas. The contrasting of Roman order and barbarian disorder through the depiction of complex, bonding military manoeuvres, including the Roman battle manoeuvre known as the *testudo*, will also be discussed. Finally, attention will be turned to images of Roman soldiers involved in head hunting, the image of the severed barbarian head being the grossest, but most effective, symbol of Roman power and the ultimate objectification of the barbarian body.

Barbarian costume and equipment

While numerous individual barbarians appear on the reliefs of the column, principally Germans and Sarmatians, the column representations cannot really usefully be used for any study of these peoples as ethnic types nor for a study of their costumes and their material equipment and weapons. Obviously some information can be gleaned on these topics, but not perhaps as much as might have been expected. Of course, the viewer can relatively easily distinguish between

Romans and barbarians, even in the upper scenes, and between one barbarian ethnic group and another to some extent, but detail is missing. The column reliefs did not provide sufficient information to satisfy one of Peteresen's avowed aims of studying the column in detail in order to gather information on the ancient German peoples and their customs.[1]

Looking at a number of images on the column the following basic descriptions can be given of the barbarians. German men are usually portrayed as bearded and with long straggly hair. Their heads are normally uncovered. They wear trousers and long tunics, usually tied around the waist by a belt; some of the tunics are fringed at the bottom. They often wear a cloak fastened at the right shoulder. Some of them wear neck torques. The previous Roman signifier for a German was to portray one wearing an animal fur or pelt of some kind. Earlier Domitianic representations of German men had often depicted the men as bare-chested and indeed one or two semi-naked figures do also appear on the column. Other than that, they differed little from the Aurelian images, though the earlier images often included more accessory detail of shoes, trousers and so on. It is interesting to note that Roman military garb was by now well advanced in its move away from the 'Roman' or 'Italian' model of the Republic and of the first and earlier second centuries, towards a transformation which Simon James has called 'a provincialisation' or 'de-Italianization'.[2] He continues:

> Military dress no longer represented the male clothing traditions of the Mediterranean core, but those of the provincial periphery and beyond: the standard 'barbarian' dress of the North and East had displaced Italian garments. Instead of a simple tunic which left the limbs bare, and various types of cloak, the soldiers now wore essentially the same garments as males (at least, free warrior males?) of the peoples along and beyond the frontiers; long-sleeved tunics, long trousers, and the northern blanket-cloak.[3]

German women mostly have long hair worn down, though some have their hair tied up and a few wear some form of cloth hair covering. It has been suggested that those women portrayed with their hair down are in mourning of some kind.[4] They wear two principal types of garment: 'a long-sleeved tunic with a sleeveless, perhaps woollen, jumper on top, tied by two belts, one at the waist and one under the breasts; and a single layer comprising a short-sleeved tunic belted below the waist, sometimes with a mantle over the back'. The German children portrayed are mostly boys, all wearing a miniature version of the men's standard belted tunic and trousers/leggings, sometimes with a small cloak. The few girls portrayed wear long drapery. The Sarmatian men normally appear in a similar military garb to the German men but with conical caps.

It is possible that accurate representation of barbarians, their costumes and equipment were not deemed to be of relevance to the overall aims of the scheme for the column or, more likely, we are seeing here a manifestation of a trend that had really begun after the reign of Trajan for not signifying barbarian identities in artworks beyond the generalities of difference which were necessary to aid the viewer's identification. A number of authorities have noted this trend on coin representations, on cuirassed statue breastplates and in monumental art.[5] The almost anthropological recording of ethnic types and their equipment for which the Augustan era in particular was noteworthy had long passed.[6] These people were not to be studied, they were to be feared. They were different, but the visual markers of their difference were to be simple, often generic indicators, rather than specific visual indicators.

On Trajan's Column, one of the first things that strikes the viewer is that there was a concerted effort by the artist to represent the Dacians as a distinct ethnic group, rather than as undifferentiated, generic barbarians, as was later to be the case in Roman art. However, there was little individuality amongst the basic Dacian types, whether male or female. So much has been written about the detailed depictions of Roman military equipment, arms and armour on the column, that it is easy to overlook the fact that the same attention to detail was not expended on the attributes of the Dacians, though the spoils in the sculptural trophy pile on the pediment of the monument are clearly recognisably Dacian armaments. In earlier times Roman art had established a distinct and direct engagement, in terms of veracity of representation, with the depiction of the Gaul or Celt and with their distinctive weaponry, something that may have reflected a different attitude to these peoples to that of the Dacians at the time of Trajan, and most certainly to the Germans during the Antonine period.

Rude huts

Scenes XCVIII and LXXXII on the column are rare examples of the representation here of Roman troops engaged in a non-combat activity, in one of these scenes the soldiers are using long-handled entrenching tools, possibly to dig ditches, and in another to build fortification walls (*71 & 72*). Such scenes of building and construction are much more common on Trajan's Column for probably quite specific reasons.[7] However, as is noted elsewhere in this volume, the use of images of buildings to denote the stark differences between Roman and barbarian is a marked theme of Marcus's column.

Scene CII depicts a Roman soldier torching huts in a German village. Two of the three huts representing the village are caught at the point where their thatched roofs have burst into flames (*73*). The torching of a village also appears in a number of other scenes on the column. It is interesting to see the way in which the designer/principal artist of the column frieze has used architecture as a signifier of the difference between Roman and non-Roman, thus between civilization and barbarism.[8] If one examines the early scenes involving the Roman army crossing the Danube, we can see that along the banks of the river, on the civilised side, there are depicted a number of buildings forming a small village or hamlet (*74*). The buildings are rectangular in plan and probably of two storeys, as there are windows

71 Roman soldiers dig ditches. Scene XCVIII. The Column of Marcus Aurelius, Rome. (Photo: Graham Norrie, after Petersen *et al.* 1896)

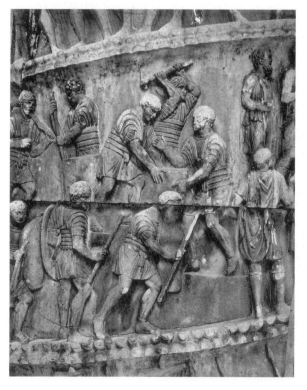

72 Roman soldiers engaged in building activity. Scene LXXXII. The Column of Marcus Aurelius, Rome. (Photo: Graham Norrie, after Petersen *et al.* 1896)

or openings at second floor level on all three houses. They all have pitched roofs. One of the buildings, the largest, would appear to be constructed of dressed stone with a tiled roof and a porticoed entrance. The building next to it would appear to be also of stone, though built of less monumentally sized blocks, and again has a tiled roof. It stands within a compound formed by a stout wooden fence and a solid wooden gate, giving access into the courtyard. The third building would appear to be of timber construction, with a thatched or shingle roof. Once more it stands within a fenced compound, the fence here being less massive than that of its neighbour. Thus we are seeing represented here the variety of Romanised buildings that constitute a civilised urban centre. As if to drill home the point about architecture and engineering being signifiers of Romanisation, as Tacitus had stated in his description of his father-in-law Agricola's governorship of Roman Britain,[9] we shortly see the Roman forces crossing an elaborate and beautifully constructed pontoon bridge over the river. The span of the bridge is massive. Its deck ably supports the weight of a long column of Roman troops, both infantry and cavalry, as they cross the frontier, its parapet of interlaced timbers preventing anyone from falling over the side of the bridge, and its arched ends serving to give the impression of a triumphal progress from civilisation to barbarity.

Further points are made about monumentality in the depiction of Roman military encampments on the column, their solidity further emphasising the

73 Simple huts in a German village being burned by Roman troops. Scene CII. The Column of Marcus Aurelius, Rome. (Photo: DAIR 55.1143)

74 Romanised buildings along the Danube and within the empire. Scene I. The Column of Marcus Aurelius, Rome. (Photo: Graham Norrie, after Petersen *et al.* 1896)

materiality, the physicality of the Roman presence. It is interesting that in Scene XI, centred on the depiction of the Miracle of the Thunderbolt and discussed in detail elsewhere, the Germans are attempting to overcome the Romans by trying to turn around the Romans' architectural superiority in the form of their impenetrable fort, by laying siege to the camp, turning the fort from an offensive monument into a defensive one. The Germans' construction of a siege tower marks their attempt to assault the very fabric, the very physicality of the Roman construction and thus challenge the superiority of Roman monumentality and thus of its cultural values.

In contrast to all of this, we have the numerous depictions on the column of native German huts. These huts are round as opposed to rectangular, something that can be seen archaeologically to mark out the difference between Roman and native in many provinces of the empire. They are small structures which would appear to be constructed of wattle and daub or of bundled reeds, with a single doorway, usually shown as open, with the door tied back to one side, and a cone-like roof. They resemble nothing so much as large upturned baskets. Two basic, almost similar, types of native hut are shown. The native stronghold depicted in Scene LIV, for instance, appears a slight, flimsy construction in comparison to the Roman forts and camps depicted. It would appear to have defences built of panels of hurdling, of intertwined branches and twigs.

The question as to whether buildings shown on the column are in any way 'accurate' in their form has been addressed by scholars who have found that the images are detailed enough to be more than simple generalisations, but not detailed enough to suggest specific, in-depth knowledge of such structures on behalf of the artists/carvers working on the column frieze.

The monumentality of the Romanised buildings on the Roman side of the Danube and that of the military pontoon bridge are echoes of the monumentality of the column itself, its massive base, its drum-like shaft soaring upwards towards the heavens, which again reflects the monumentality of its setting and thus of Rome itself. Architecture and buildings were indeed expressions of Roman imperialism, but more than that they played 'an often pivotal role in "materializing" imperial ideologies and coercion, as the most visible means through which to present the Roman state, a social construction, physically throughout the empire'.[10]

It is interesting to note in this context that the decorative scene on one of so-called legionary distance slabs from Hutcheson Hill, Bearsden on the Antonine Wall in Scotland, set up by the *Legio* XX in the 140s AD, also uses the motif of a classical-style building and a classical deity to provide contrast with the figures of defeated barbarians here.[11] The scene on the slab contains an elaborately designed architectural setting, either a temple or, more likely, a triumphal arch, with figures placed in the central arched space and in the pedimented spaces on either side. The central scene depicts Victory crowning a member of the triumphant Roman forces, in this case a standard-bearer, while looking on from the sides are two bound barbarian captives, the line of their gaze suggesting that they are viewers of the victory ceremony.

It was not only the opposition of barbarity to civilisation that was indicated by the depiction of native huts on the column used as juxtaposed images to Romanised buildings. The organic nature of these huts, built of wood, wattle and daub, reeds or rushes, gave them an in-built obsolescence, a temporal limit, as opposed to the implied permanence of the stouter-looking Romanised structures. The Roman Empire, this implied, would last. These barbarian cultures, while they might now be virile and a threat to Rome, would eventually decay like rotting wood.

Field manoeuvres

It has already been noted elsewhere in this volume that the artistic programme of the column repeatedly used images to stress the order and discipline of the Roman army and the chaotic disorder of their barbarian opponents. This difference can be seen in the structuring and appearance of the numerous battle scenes that were discussed in detail in Chapter Seven. This sense of order, again part of the overall strategy of managing difference, was particularly stressed by two scenes in which the Roman troops were depicted carrying out complex military manoeuvres which emphasised their cohesion and organisation.

In the first of these scenes, Scene LIV on the column, a cohort of Roman soldiers is portrayed forming a *testudo* – a tortoise – forming a protective canopy of shields above and around themselves so as to fend off enemy missiles and to move forward in unison against the enemy (75). This particular orchestrated field manoeuvre is described by Livy and thus is likely to have been well known to many Romans, both military and civilian. This manoeuvre is also represented in Scene LXXI on Trajan's Column and it is likely that the occurrence of such a scene on both columns, once only on each, is more than a simple coincidence. On the Aurelian column we see the enemy raining missiles down onto the advancing *testudo*, including swords, a helmet, a lighted torch or brand, and even a cart or chariot wheel, all to no avail as the formation of interlocked shields holds firm.

75 A testudo engaged in fighting. Scene LIV. The Column of Marcus Aurelius, Rome. (Photo: Graham Norrie, after Petersen *et al.* 1896)

Once more the materiality of this instant shelter as protection for the Roman troops who have drilled to perform this manoeuvre through constant training is visual evidence of the superiority of Roman arms and Roman civilisation. Cassius Dio in fact alludes to the Roman forces 'fighting valiantly with their shields locked together' in his description of the events leading up to the Miracle of the Rains as if their adoption here of this formation sets them apart from their Germanic foes.[12]

The second scene involving a military manoeuvre, which may have been visible from the ground because of its size and composition even though it is high up on the column shaft, involves a squadron of Roman cavalry (Scene CIII) (*76*) pictured at a gallop, wheeling around in a circle, probably to form up in line behind a procession of infantry troops. This scene is so similar to the two *decursio* scenes on the base of the Column of Antoninus Pius, discussed in Chapter Two, that it is difficult to believe that the artist here was not making a conscious reference to this earlier image. There might even have been some allusion here to the future *decursio* that would be held for Marcus ahead of his cremation and apotheosis.

76 Roman cavalry wheel around and form up. Scene CIII. The Column of Marcus Aurelius, Rome. (Photo: Graham Norrie, after Petersen *et al.* 1896)

A severed head

Head hunting by Roman soldiers can be seen in Scenes LXVI and LXIV/LXV (*77 & 78*) on Marcus's column, one scene showing heads being brought before Marcus (*77*) and another showing a barbarian man being decapitated (*78*), a bloodthirsty activity that is also well-attested on Trajan's Column. There has been much discussion of the significance of this practice, and it is perhaps curious that its representation appears on both columns, although the duplication of a number of Trajanic column images, albeit in sometimes different ways, on the Aurelian column is noteworthy. Once more, in this context it is worth recalling the historically attested appalling post-mortem treatment of the severed head and hand of the Dacian king, Decebalus, in order to try to understand the significance of these acts of ritualised bodily dismemberment in the context of the wider study of fragmentation of the body in Roman art.[13]

While in Greek society and art the body remained an almost inviolable whole, in Roman art the body became something that could sometimes be portrayed

77 A severed head of a barbarian is presented to the emperor. Scene LXVI. The Column of Marcus Aurelius, Rome. (Photo: Graham Norrie, after Petersen *et al.* 1896)

78 Barbarian
prisoners, one of
whom is possibly
being decapitated
in the background.
Scene LXIV/LXV. The
Column of Marcus
Aurelius, Rome.
(Photo: Graham
Norrie, after Petersen
et al. 1896)

simply by representing the head or bust of an individual. The cropping of images
of people often occurred in wall paintings and on gemstones. Body parts of
statues were sometimes intentionally interchangeable by design. Portrait heads
could be re-carved, sometimes out of economic necessity, other times for more
political reasons. The sick could represent themselves at healing shrines with *ex
votos* portraying their diseased or affected body parts. The human body in these
instances was not simply modified, it was transformed into a series of unrelated
parts. There was evidently a tension between beliefs in Roman society, mirrored
in Roman culture, of the body as an ideal form and the body as a flexible image.
Marcus Aurelius himself in the *Meditations* muses on the wholeness of the physical
body and of the social body and how each can become fragmented.[14]

This fragmentation of the body when it occurred perhaps reflected a
permeability of boundaries in Roman society and culture, particularly between life
and death, and sickness and health. The social body in certain contexts condoned
and acquiesced in this dismemberment of the corporeal body into images. In
some instances the corporeal body was reduced to the status of an artefact.

In thinking about analysing the fragmented body, consideration needs to be given to psychoanalytical approaches to the viewing and reception of fragmented and fragmentary images of the body, approaches principally championed by Melanie Klein and Jacques Lacan, and in the field of classics by Page Dubois.[15] The psychoanalyst and social theorist Julia Kristeva has been involved in an art-historical research project, centred on the exhibition '*Visions Capitales*' held at the Louvre in 1998 and its accompanying catalogue of the same name. Through an exploration of the image of the severed or disassociated head from prehistoric contexts up to its inclusion in the art of Andy Warhol in the 1960s, the project provides a broad context for aiding understanding of the varying cultural situations in which the image has been employed.[16]

As has been noted elsewhere in this volume, the Roman headhunting scenes and scenes of beheadings discussed here should perhaps be seen in the wider context of Roman attitudes towards the games and towards judicial punishment. It is worth recalling also that Dio Cassius records a number of instances of imperially sanctioned head hunting for a bounty during the Marcomannic wars. In the first instance he tells how Marcus was particularly bitter towards Ariogaesus, king of the *Quadi*, so that in AD 173, 'he issued a proclamation to the effect that anyone who brought him in alive should receive a thousand gold pieces, and anyone who slew him and exhibited his head, five hundred'.[17] In the second instance Dio recounts how in AD 175 Marcus was marching against the usurper Cassius when he was met by some of his men who had killed Cassius 'and cut off his head'. Marcus 'was so greatly aggrieved at the death of Cassius that he could not bring himself even to look at the severed head of his enemy, but before the murderers drew near gave orders that it should be buried'.[18]

Touching from a Distance

In this volume the Column of Marcus Aurelius and its decorated spiral or helical frieze have been discussed at length. The physical form of the column has been described and its ancient setting has been reconstructed, as far as that is possible. The original, now-replaced, base of the monument has been described as recorded by sixteenth-century antiquarian illustrators and its simple, uncomplicated message as conveyed by the artworks on it has been discussed. The frieze has also been analysed in terms of its programmatic design and the way in which the ancient viewer might have been expected to interact with the monument, and what they might have been intended to learn from looking at the frieze in the piecemeal manner that its design necessitated. The way in which scholars of ancient art have studied the column and the way that these studies have often been influenced by contemporary academic fashions and by advances in technology have also been touched upon.

A full photographic record of the column's frieze allows us to examine the whole design of the frieze and in intimate detail, in a way that was never envisaged by the frieze's designer. However, this does not allow us to read the frieze from beginning to end, or rather from bottom to top, or to reconstruct a complete narrative from what we see represented there. The frieze does not have a story as such: it is not a documentary record of Marcus's Marcomannic wars. It does allude to those wars in its many scenes of battle and carnage but, again, many of these scenes are generic and are intended to convey messages not linked to historical specifity. An exception to this is provided by the depictions of the two so-called Weather Miracles, both historically attested, whose individual significance has been discussed above at length.

The column is not, then, a triumphal monument, it is a funerary monument, something stressed by its positioning in the *Campus Martius* in Rome, and one dedicated to the memory of Marcus Aurelius and his wife Faustina, if an inscription relating to the monument is to be accepted. But, and this is a considerable but, their memory was mediated through the mind and motives of Marcus's son Commodus, who would appear to have been keen to use the monument as a reflection of his own position in the scheme of Roman imperial ideology. Commodus, by his sanction of the monument in both its form and its artistic programme, stressed his blood link to Marcus and the legitimacy of his rule following an era of adopted emperors. He helped cast Marcus, some years after his death, as the new Trajan, a soldier-emperor (79), and did this by linking the column of Marcus to that of Trajan in its form, its decoration, its setting, the repetition and copying of some of its themes of decoration, and so on. It was not a copy of Trajan's Column, it was a reflection of it.

The frieze on Marcus's column was not a poorer piece of art than the frieze on Trajan's Column, it was simply different, in terms of its conception and style and in its execution. In many ways the Aurelian frieze was a better work of art, in that it was a more efficient vehicle than Trajan's frieze for promoting the ideas of its sponsor to the various audiences of viewers in Rome.

The viewers' emotions were intended to be manipulated to a great extent by many of the images on the column frieze, but how far this manipulation succeeded would have depended on who was viewing the column and how they were viewing it. It is almost universally agreed that certain images could be more easily viewed from the ground than others, and an attempt has been made to reflect this accessibility of certain individual images and repeated types of images

79 Marcus on the Danube bridge. Scene LXXVIII. The Column of Marcus Aurelius, Rome. (Photo: Graham Norrie, after Petersen *et al.* 1896)

in the weighting of their discussion in the chapters above. Most viewers would have been able to understand the simple messages of the artworks on the column base and to read the dedicatory inscription, and then might have spent time looking at the column and walking around it to view the frieze from a number of standpoints, from where they would have been able to see the early scenes involving the river god overseeing the crossing of the Danube (*80*) and the two extraordinary depictions of the Weather Miracles. It is likely that other images could be relatively easily spotted, including those scenes involving the emperor which were both vertically arranged and probably highlighted in some way by colouring or gilding, the giant figure of the semi-nude Victory and possibly the Roman fighting *testudo* formation of interlocked shields. Other types of scenes might have been picked out because of their repetitive use, scenes such as battles, the mistreatment of barbarian women, and scenes of pathetic barbarians in defeat. Many of the images would simply have been unviewable in any coherent way, particularly at the very top of the column, where farm animals wander off into the distance across a landscape of stylised trees (*81*).

80 The river god of the Danube benevolently overseeing the Roman crossing of the river. Scene III. The Column of Marcus Aurelius, Rome. (Photo: Graham Norrie, after Petersen *et al.* 1896)

81 Stray domestic animals wander back to the fields. Scene CXVI. The Column of Marcus Aurelius, Rome. (Photo: Graham Norrie, after Petersen *et al.* 1896)

The column frieze most certainly has a sub-text of what might be called ultra-violence, and beneath that a further subtext relating to violence against women and the eroticisation of violence. How many of the violent scenes would have been accessible to viewers must remain unknown to us, and whether the numerous depictions of women suffering on the column were appreciated as making some specific point again cannot be gauged. Just as the artworks on the column as a whole need to be studied in the broader context of Roman imperial art in general, and in the context of Antonine art in particular, so these violent images perhaps can only really be understood as part of a broader study of the place of violence in Roman society. Images of suffering bodies were maps whose reading confirmed to the Romans their place at the centre of the world.

Finally, the violent images on the column have been considered more broadly as part of a general pattern and acceptance of institutionalised violence in Roman society, as reflected, for example, in certain kinds of judicial punishments and in the games in the arena, and of depictions of pain and suffering in other contexts, both ancient and modern. It has been discussed whether the modern western

82 The Roman
forces march across
a pontoon bridge.
Scene CVIII. The
Column of Marcus
Aurelius, Rome.
(Photo: Graham
Norrie, after Petersen
et al. 1896)

viewer's generally empathetic response to images of suffering has preconditioned
or distorted our reading of these ancient images.

New dawn fades

It has been constantly stressed throughout the book how, from the time of
Marcus Aurelius and Commodus onwards, there was a highly noticeable and
significant trend in Roman imperial art towards the growing dehumanisation
of the barbarian, through the sometimes highly graphic depiction of their fate
at the hands of Roman troops. The extraordinarily harrowing and ultra-violent
scenes of slaughter and carnage on the Column of Marcus Aurelius in Rome
represent the most extreme manifestation of this trend. Before the time of Trajan,
the direct depiction of battle on monuments in Rome itself was rare, though
in the Augustan and Julio-Claudian eras such scenes of warfare appeared quite
widely on monuments in the provinces, and it was probably on Trajan's Column

83 The Roman forces carry their equipment in a baggage train. Scene CXI. The Column of Marcus Aurelius, Rome. (Photo: Graham Norrie, after Petersen *et al.* 1896)

84 Marcus in consultation with his staff officers as battle rages on nearby. Scene XIX. The Column of Marcus Aurelius, Rome. (Photo: Graham Norrie, after Petersen *et al.* 1896)

that the extensive depiction of battle scenes first occurred. On the Column of Marcus Aurelius scenes of the army at work or on the march were few (*82 & 83*) and battle dominated the helical frieze to an even greater extent, (*84*) and this also occurred in the private funerary art – the battle sarcophagi – associated with some senior military figures in the army of the time. The development of this trend, of course, reflected broader changes within certain sections of Roman society at the time, including changes in the value-system of many of those aristocratic Romans involved in public life.

The trend can also be seen in Roman military art, such as on the legionary distance slabs from the Antonine Wall in Scotland, and some authorities have argued that the debasement and dehumanisation of the barbarian had its origins in the military rather than the political sphere, occurring in military art at a much earlier period. The figure of the barbarian thus became a convenient canvas on which the fears and neuroses of the Roman state were indelibly drawn. There was to be no return to the ambiguity in the depiction of Rome's enemies of previous eras, nor was the idealisation of the primitive again to be part of the Roman imperial rhetoric of power. These were, in fact, all different strategies employed by Rome in its management of difference and part of the ideology which underpinned Roman cultural identity. Constant trouble on the frontiers from the later second century onwards, and the pressure of fighting defensive war after defensive war, gradually eroded Roman self confidence and this was reflected, or rather deflected, in the bluster of much imperial art of the later empire. It was not the case that the Roman attitude to barbarians at this time reflected a xenophobic attitude towards any of the barbarian peoples portrayed in the art of the time,[1] it was simply that in the Roman psyche there was a genuine fear of many of the barbarian peoples beyond the frontiers, even though the barbarianisation of the Roman army continued apace throughout the period.

Victory against barbarian foes may no longer have been enough in itself, as two rather different examples, one textual and one artefactual, will demonstrate. Cassius Dio tells us that Marcus Aurelius 'both because he knew their race [the Iazyges] to be untrustworthy and also because he had been deceived by the Quadi, wished to annihilate them utterly'.[2] A similar attitude and similarly apocalyptic vocabulary can be found on a metal dice shaker for gaming found at a *villa rustica,* probably owned by an ex-military man, at Vettweip-Froitzheim in Germany, inscribed with the words PICTOS VICTOS HOSTIS DELETA LUDITE SECURI – 'the Picts are beaten, the enemy annihilated, let us play without a care'.[3]

If the desperate and vicious battle scenes on the Column of Marcus do then represent a reflection in stone of the stress of the era, brought on by the growth of fear of the barbarian, then one might expect to find other contemporary manifestations of this Roman malaise, some state reaction to public fear. It has been suggested that just such a reading can be made of the coinage of the era, adorned with repetitive slogans of reassurance –*Aeternitas, Securitas, Fortuna,*

85 A messenger
arrives at
Marcus's camp.
Scene CI.
The Column
of Marcus
Aurelius, Rome.
(Photo: Graham
Norrie, after
Petersen *et al.*
1896)

Spes, Providentia, Felicitas Temporum, and so on – slogans that promised peace, tranquility and eternal Roman rule.[4] There was no better medium to get across the message than by the use of simple slogan on items as ubiquitous as coins, objects so accessible to so many people in a way that monuments could never be.

Towards the top of the Column of Marcus Aurelius, in a scene that was probably highlighted for the benefit of the contemporary Roman viewer as it included the figure of the emperor, a messenger dramatically races into a Roman camp (Scene CI) (*85*). His speed is indicated by the billowing out of his cloak as he approaches his goal, his body twisting to one side to negotiate the probably clavicular entrance and deliver some important message to the emperor. Why the need for such urgency we do not know. Who he is and where he has come from we also do not know. Who sent him and what his message was we can only guess. All these things are ultimately unknowable to us and must remain as enigmatic to modern viewers as the Column of Marcus Aurelius itself.

Notes

Preface

1 Ammianus Marcellinus 31.8.5.

Chapter One: Meditations on War

1 This summary of Marcus's life is primarily based on the definitive biography, revised edition, by Anthony Birley – Birley 1987. On Marcus see also Farquharson 1951, Görlitz 1954, Grimal 1991, Klein 1979, Renan 1923, Rosen 1997, Schall 1991, Stemmer 1988 and Wegner 1938.
2 Cassius Dio 71.36.4. Translation by E. Cary 1927, reprinted in The Loeb Classical Library edition of 1955.
3 Birley 1987, 211.
4 Birley 1987, 212.
5 *Meditations* 4.3. Translation by A.S.L. Farquharson 1944, reproduced in Oxford World Classics 2008.
6 *Meditations* 2.2.
7 *Meditations* 8.34.
8 *Meditations* 4.21.
9 On the dimensions and built form of the column see Claridge 1998, 193–196, Gatti in Caprino *et al.* 1955 and particularly Martines 2000.
10 Claridge 1998, 193–196.
11 Panzanelli 2008.
12 Bianchi Bandinelli 2003.
13 Durnan 2000, 34.
14 Beckmann 2005 and Claridge 2005.
15 Beckmann 2005, 303.
16 Beckmann 2005, 303.
17 Beckmann 2005, 303.
18 Beckmann 2005, 309.
19 Beckmann 2005, 312.
20 Claridge 2005.
21 On antiquarian illustrations of the column see, for instance, Colini 1954, Colini in Caprino *et al.* 1955, Davies 2000, 45–46 and various papers in Scheid and Huet 2000, particularly Huet 2000.

22 Jordan-Ruwe 1990.
23 CIL 6.1585 and Colini in Caprino *et al.* 1955, 38–41.
24 On the 1589 renovations see, for instance, Colini in Caprino *et al.* 1955, 35–36, Davies 2000, 45–46 and Martines 2000, 64–68.
25 Colini 1955.
26 Davies 2000. On the significance of the *Campus Martius* see also Castagnoli 1947, Jolivet 1988 and Von Domaszewski 1909.
27 Davies 2000, 165.
28 On the role of statues in Roman society in general see Gregory 1994 and Stewart 2003.
29 Davies 2000, 166–169.
30 Davies 2000, 170.
31 Davies 2000, 166.
32 Davies 2000, 2.
33 Davies 2000, 4.
34 Davies 2000, 171.
35 On the base of the Column of Antoninus Pius, see principally Davies 2000, 40–42, 99–100, 118–119 and 163–165, Kleiner 1992, 285–288 and Vogel 1973.
36 Kleiner 1992, 273–277.
37 On Commodus as Hercules see, for instance, Kleiner 1992, 276–277.
38 On the column in general see Becatti 1957 and 1960, Caprino *et al.* 1955, Ferris 2000, 86–98, Fuhrmann 1937, Hölscher 2000, Kleiner 1992, 295–301, Maffei 1993 and 1996, Morris 1952, Petersen *et al.* 1896, Pirson 1996, Scheid and Huet 2000, Strong 1961, 56–58, Zanker 2000 and Zwikker 1941.
39 On the issue of the photographic record see principally Beard 2000 and Huet 2000, 118–121. On the same issue in relation to Trajan's Column see Huet 1996.
40 On this issue see most recently Beard 2000, 267.
41 Bianchi Bandinelli 1950, 1970 and 2003.
42 The comparison of scenes on Trajan's Column to cinematic styling is most marked in Lepper and Frere 1988.
43 See Elsner 2000 for a full discussion of the frontality issue and a full bibilography.
44 On the *Stilwandel* see especially Wegner 1931 and for a broad discussion of the *Stilwandel* and the Column of Marcus Aurelius see Elsner 2000.
45 Beard 2000 and Huet 2000, 118–121.
46 Beard 2000, 265–266.
47 On the background to the *Mostra Augustea della Romanita* see Feinstein 2003 and Visser 1992.

Chapter Two: To Honour Famous Men

1 On Trajan's Column principally see Ampolo 1995, Baumer 1991, Becatti 1960, Bianchi Bandinelli 2003, Bode 1992, Brilliant 1984, 90–123, Claridge 1993, Coarelli 2000, Condurachi 1982, Coulston 1990 and 2009, Currie 1996, Davies 2000, 27–34, 85–86, 131–133 and 165–166, Dillon 2006, Ferris 2000, 61–68, Huet 1996, Kampen 1991, Kleiner 1992, 212–220, Koeppel 2002, Lepper and Frere 1988, Martines 2000, Richmond 1982, Rossi 1971 and 1978, Settis 1985 and 1988, Uzzi 2005, 123–127, Vulpe 1973, Wilson-Jones 1993 and Zanker 2000.

2 See, for instance, Kleiner 1992, 214.
3 Vogel 1973.
4 Vogel 1973, 26.
5 On the base of the Column of Antoninus Pius see principally Davies 2000, 40–42, 99–100, 118–119 and 163–165, Kleiner 1992, 285–288 and Vogel 1973.
6 On this apotheosis scene see, for instance, Davies 2000, 105–106 and 116–118, Kleiner 1992, 253–255 and Vogel 1973, 47–48.
7 Davies 2000, 166–169.
8 Lepper and Frere 1988, 187–192 and Kleiner 1992, 215.
9 On Trajan's Forum see Packer 1997.
10 Particularly in Lepper and Frere 1988.
11 Brilliant 1984, 102 and 114.
12 Kampen 1991, 219–220.
13 Brilliant 1984, 103 and 105.
14 On the suicide of Decebalus see, for instance, Ferris 2000, 68 and 80–81.
15 On the women torturers see Dillon 2006, 263–267 and Ferris 2000, 66–68.
16 On the obsessive building of camps and fortifications see, in particular, Coulston 1990.
17 Concentration on the army on the column is most marked in Richmond 1982 and Lepper and Frere 1988.
18 On headhunting see Ferris 2000, 68 and 2007, 119–121 and Rossi 1981 and in this volume Chapter eight pp. 160–162.
19 On women on Trajan's Column see Kampen 1995, Dillon 2006, 244–271, Ferris 2000, 66–68 and Zanker 2000.
20 Ferris 2000.
21 On Trajan 'the ageless adult' see, for instance Kleiner 1992, 208–212.

Chapter Three: The Fifth Good Emperor

1 Brilliant 1984, 114.
2 Brilliant 1984, 114.
3 Brilliant 1984, 114.
4 Brilliant 1984, 115.
5 Brilliant 1984, 115–116.
6 Brilliant 1994, 279.
7 Brilliant 1994, 280–281.
8 Pirson 1996.
9 An approach personified by Scheid and Huet 2000.
10 Ryberg 1955.
11 Ryberg 1955, 114 and 127. For a detailed study of the religious rites on the column see Scheid 2000.
12 Sauron 2000.
13 Brilliant 1984, 114.
14 Elsner 2000, 264.
15 Davies 2000, 171.

16 Kleiner 1992, 270.

17 Kleiner 1992, 271–273.

18 Details from the BBC News website. I am grateful to my friend Julian Parker for first drawing my attention to this discovery.

19 On the panel reliefs see, for example, Angelicoussis 1984, Kleiner 1992, 288–295, La Rocca 1986 and Ryberg 1967.

20 A suggestion made, for instance, by Kleiner 1992, 294.

21 For an illustration of the *Aquincum* mould, see Ferris 2000, 101 Plate 50.

22 On the treatment of barbarians on the Great Antonine Altar see Ferris 2000, 102–104 and on the Antonine Wall legionary distance slabs see Ferris 1994, 25–26 and 2000, 113–118.

23 On the Tripoli arch see Kleiner 1992, 308–309.

24 On the significance of the missing trampled barbarian from Marcus's equestrian statue see Ferris 2000, 99–100. On the statue in general see Sommella 1990 and Sommella and Presicce 1997.

Chapter Four: A Hard Rain

1 On the Bath head see, for instance, Cunliffe and Fulford 1982, 11 Nos. 32–37.

2 As discussed in Ryberg 1955.

3 On the Weather Miracles see Barta 1968, Berwig 1970, Birley 1987, 171–174, Fowden 1987, Guey 1948a and 1948b, Israelowich 2008 (which appeared too late to be used here), Jobst 1978, Klein 1991, Maffei 1990, Roos 1943, Rubin 1979 and Sage 1987. On the dating of the column see principally Jordan-Ruwe 1990, Morris 1952 and Sakowski 1988. On the dating of various events in the Marcomannic wars in general see the above, plus Birley 1987, 249–255, Dodd 1913, Kerr 1995 and Wolff 1994.

4 *Vita Marci* 24.4.

5 Cassius Dio 71.8–10.

6 Fowden 1987, 87–88 and Rubin 1979, 368–369.

7 Birley 1987, 173, Fowden 1987, 87–89 and Rubin 1979, 358–361. On the coinage of Marcus in general, see Dobias 1932, Foss 1990, 133–144.

8 As quoted by Fowden 1987, 85.

9 Fowden 1987, 87.

10 Fowden 1987, 90–94.

11 Fowden 1987, 93–94.

12 Birley 1987, 173 and Sage 1987.

13 Birley 1987, 173 and Rubin 1979, 365–366.

14 Walters 1984.

15 Ferris 2000, 39–48 and 69–70.

16 Walters 1984, 425.

17 Kousser 2006, 238. On Jupiter in Roman imperial ideology see Fears 1981.

18 Green 1991, 92.

19 Clarke 2004.

20 Quoted in Clarke 2004, 238.

Chapter Five: The Scream

1 Beard 2000, 276.
2 Beard 2000, 276.
3 Beard 2000, 277–278.
4 Elsner 2000, 257.
5 See, for instance Aldrete 1999, Brilliant 1963 and Corbeill 2004.
6 Aldrete 1999, 9 and 11.
7 Bianchi Bandinelli 1969, 342.
8 Bianchi Bandinelli 1969, 342.
9 Ferris 1994, 25–26 and 2000, 113–118.
10 For Mulvey's gaze theories see Mulvey 1975 and 1989. For the gaze in ancient art see, for instance, Fredrick 2002.
11 Barton 1989, 1993 and 1994.
12 See, for instance, Rawson 1987 and Weis 1992.
13 On violence, spectacle and the arena see, for instance, Auguet 1972, Beacham 1999, Coleman 1990, Futrell 1997, Hopkins 1983, Kohne and Ewigleben 2000, Kyle 1998, Lintott 1968, Plass 1995, Potter and Mattingly 1998 and Wiedemann 1992.
14 Barton 1993, 13.
15 Barton 1993, 13.
16 MacMullen 1986. On crime and punishment see also Bauman 1996.
17 MacMullen 1986, 209.
18 MacMullen 1986, 211–212.
19 MacMullen 1986, 212.
20 See, for instance, Spivey 2001 and his extensive bibliography.
21 For references to studies of Medieval and later pain and suffering in these areas see Ferris 2006, 84 and bibliography.
22 Brilliant 2002, 506. Zanker also makes use of a modern analogy to Roman violence against barbarian peoples in the form of a photograph of an atrocity in Sarajevo – Zanker 2002, 38 Plate 22.
23 Spivey 2000, 237.
24 Ferguson 1980 and Gore 1987.
25 Ferguson 1980, 73.
26 James 2002.
27 Gilliver 1995.
28 For instance, Carman 1997. For other references see Ferris 2006, 88 and bibliography.

Chapter Six: Power and Gender

1 The possibility of there having been statues of both Marcus and Faustina is broached by, for instance, Hannestad 1988, 237.
2 Hassall 1977, 338.
3 Hassall 1977, 340 Note 34.
4 For Faustina on the *adventus* panel relief see Kleiner 1992, 291.
5 Hassall 1977, 336–338.
6 Hassall 1977, 338.

7 Kousser 2006 and on Victory more generally particularly Goulaki-Voutira 1992 and Hölscher 1967 and 2006.
8 Kousser 2006, 224–227.
9 On Mars and Venus portrait groups see Kleiner 1981 and Kousser 2006, 227–228. The quotation is from Kousser 2006, 227.
10 Kousser 2006, 228–229.
11 On women on Marcus's column and on Trajan's Column see Kampen 1995, Dillon 2006, 244–271, Ferris 2000, 66–68 and Zanker 2000.
12 On images of barbarian women in general see Ferris 2000, 38–39 and 92–98 and bibliography and Rodgers 2003.
13 Ferris 2000, 36–38.
14 On the interpretation of the Claudius and *Britannia* relief, see Ferris 1994, 26–27 and 2000, 55–58 and 166–167, Webster 1997, 174–175 and Vout 2007, 25–26.
15 Kunze 1992, 31 Fig. 22.
16 On Petersen's joke see Beard 2000.
17 Beard 2000, 266–267.
18 On the women torturers see Dillon 2006, 263–267 and Ferris 2000, 66–68.
19 Uzzi 2005, 129–135.
20 See Note 11.
21 Dillon 2006, 262.
22 Cassius Dio 71.2–3.
23 Ferris 2000, 38–39, 72–74 and 167–168.
24 See Note 12.
25 On Tarpeia see Ferris 2000, 31–32 and 165 and Kampen 1991.
26 On Arachne see D'Ambra 1993 and Ferris 2000, 165–166.
27 Kellum 1996.
28 Kellum 1996, 170.

Chapter Seven: Hate and War

1 Pirson 1996, 140.
2 Pirson 1996, 155.
3 Pirson 1996. For other studies on Roman violence in warfare see also, for instance, Goldsworthy 1996, Hannestad 2001, Harris 2005, Holscher 2000, James Forthcoming and Timonen 2000. Balty 2000 and David 2000 concentrate on the Roman military on Marcus's column.
4 Pirson 1996, 140.
5 Pirson 1996, 158.
6 Pirson 1996, 159.
7 Pirson 1996, 159.
8 Pirson 1996, 161.
9 On the Bridgeness legionary distance slab see Ferris 1994, 25–26 and 2000, 113–115.
10 Ferris 2000, 115.
11 On the Orange arch see Ferris 2000, 53 and on the Adamklissi monument see Ferris 2000, 69–70.

12 Ferris 2000, 105–113 and 125–127 and Kleiner 1992, 301–303 and 388–390.
13 Kleiner 1992, 388–390.
14 Strong 1961, 99.
15 Kleiner 1992, 302.
16 Kleiner 1992, 301–302.
17 Kampen 1981.
18 *Vita Marci* 22.6–8.
19 Ferris 2000, 160–162.
20 Ferris 2000, 154–155.
21 On the Antonine Wall legionary distance slabs see Ferris 1994, 25–26 and 2000, 113–118.
22 Ferris 1994, 25–26 and 2000, 113–115.
23 Ferris 2000, 155–160.
24 Pirson 1996, 162.
25 Beard 2000, 266 Note 9.

Chapter Eight: Managing Difference

1 Beard 2000, 265–266 Note 5.
2 James 1999, 21.
3 James 1999, 21–22.
4 Zanker 2000.
5 For barbarians on coins see Levi 1952 and on cuirassed statue breastplates see Gergel 1994.
6 Ferris 2000, 6–13.
7 Coulston 1990.
8 Coulston 1990 and Hanoune 2000.
9 Tacitus *Agricola* 21.
10 Häussler 1999, 1.
11 Ferris 2000, 116–117 and Hassall 1977, 327–330.
12 Cassius Dio 71.14.
13 On the head of Decebalus see Ferris 2000, 68 and 80–81. On the fragmentary image in Roman art see Ferris 2003 and 2007.
14 *Meditations* 8.34.
15 Dubois 1996 and Ferris 2007.
16 Kristeva 1998.
17 Cassius Dio 71.14.
18 Cassius Dio 71.27–28.

Chapter Nine: Touching from a Distance

1 Ferris 2000, 162–165.
2 Cassius Dio 71.7.
3 Ferris 2000, 163.
4 Hölscher 2000, 103–105.

Bibliography

Many of the major sources on the Column of Marcus Aurelius are in Italian, German and French. Although this book is aimed at an English-speaking audience, a number of these foreign language references are included in this bibliography in order to allow the reader to follow these up, should he or she so desire.

On the subject of barbarians in Roman art, a topic much discussed in this book, readers are directed to the very full bibliography included in *Enemies of Rome. Barbarians Through Roman Eyes* (Ferris 2001). In order to avoid unnecessary duplication, only a few key references to sources on barbarians have been included in this present book.

Aillagon, J-J. (ed.) 2008 *Roma e i Barbari. La Nascita di un Nuovo Mondo*. Skira, Milan

Aldrete, G.S. 1999 *Gestures and Acclamation in Ancient Rome*. Johns Hopkins University Press, Baltimore

Ampolo, C. 1995 'L'Omen Victoriae della Colonna Traiana' *Archeologia Classica* 47, 317–327

Angelicoussis, E. 1984 'The Panel Reliefs of Marcus Aurelius' *Mitteilungen des Deutschen Archäologischen Instituts, Römische Abteilung* 91, 141–205

Auguet, R. 1972 *Cruelty and Civilization: the Roman Games*. Allen and Unwin, London

Baker, P., Forcey, C., Jundi, S. and Witcher, R. (eds) 1999 *TRAC 98 Proceedings of the Eighth Annual Theoretical Roman Archaeology Conference Leicester 1998*. Oxbow Books, Oxford

Balty, J. 2000 'L'Armée de la Colonne Aurélienne: Images de la Cohésion d'un Corps' in Scheid, J. and Huet, V. (eds) 2000, 197–204

Barta, G. 1968 'Legende und Wirklichkeit – das Regenwunder des Marcus Aurelius' *Acta Classica Universitatis Scientiarum* IV, 85–91

Barton, C.A. 1989 'The Scandal of the Arena' *Representations* 27, 1–36

Barton, C.A. 1993 *The Sorrows of the Ancient Romans. The Gladiator and the Monster*. Princeton University Press, Princeton, New Jersey

Barton, C.A. 1994 'Savage Miracles: the Redemption of Lost Honor in Roman Society and the Sacrament of the Gladiator and the Martyr' *Representations* 45, 41–71

Bauman, R.A. 1996 *Crime and Punishment in Ancient Rome*. Routledge, London

Baumer, L., Hölscher, T. and Winkler, L. 1991 'Narrative Systematik und Politisches Konzept in den Reliefs der Traianssäule' *Jahrbuch des Deutschen Archäologischen Instituts* 106, 261–295

Beacham, R.C. 1999 *Power into Pageantry: Spectacle Entertainments of Early Imperial Rome.* Yale University Press, New Haven

Beard, M. 2000 'The Spectator and the Column: Reading and Writing the Language of Gesture' in Scheid, J. and Huet, V. (eds) 2000, 265–279

Becatti, G. 1957 *La Colonna di Marco Aurelio.* Editoriale Domus, Milan

Becatti, G. 1960 *La Colonna Coclide Istoriata: Problemi Storici, Iconografici, Stilistici.* L'Erma di Bretschneider, Rome

Beckmann, M. 2005 'The Border of the Frieze of the Column of Marcus Aurelius and its Implications' *Journal of Roman Archaeology* 18 Fasc. 1, 303–312

Berwig, D. 1970 'Die Archäologische Darstellung des Regenwunders' in Berwig, D. (ed.) 1970 *Mark Aurel und die Christen*, 151–157. Sockng/Starnberg, Nowotny

Bianchi Bandinelli, R. 1950 *Storicità dell'arte classica.* Electa, Florence

Bianchi Bandinelli, R. 1969 *Roma. L'arte Romana nel centro del potere.* Rizzoli, Milan

Bianchi Bandinelli, R. 2003 *Il maestro delle imprese di Traiano.* Electa, Milan

Birley, A. 1987 *Marcus Aurelius: a Biography.* Revised edition. Batsford, London

Bode, R. 1992 'Der Bilderfries der Traianssäule' *Bonner Jahrbücher* 192, 123–174

Brilliant, R. 1963 'Gesture and Rank in Roman Art' *Memoirs of the Connecticut Academy of Arts and Sciences vol.* XIV. New Haven, Connecticut

Brilliant, R. 1984 *Visual Narratives: Storytelling in Etruscan and Roman Art.* Cornell University Press, Ithaca

Brilliant, R. 1994 'Temporal Aspects of Late Roman Art' reprinted in Brilliant, R. 1994 *Commentaries on Roman Art*, 273–296. Pindar Press, London

Brilliant, R. 2002 'The Column of Marcus Aurelius Re-Viewed' *Journal of Roman Archaeology* 15 Fasc. 2, 499–506

Campbell, J.B. 1984 *The Emperor and the Roman Army.* Oxford University Press, Oxford

Caprino, C., Colini, A.M., Gatti, G., Pallottino, M. and Romanelli, P. 1955 *La Colonna di Marco Aurelio.* L'Erma di Bretschneider, Milan

Carman, J. (ed.) 1997 *Material Harm. Archaeological Studies of War and Violence.* Cruithne Press, Glasgow

Castagnoli, F. 1947 'Il Campo Marzo nell'antichità. Memorie' *Atti della Accademia Nazionale dei Lincei, Classe di Scienze Morali, Storiche e Filosogiche* 8.1, 93–193

Claridge, A. 1993 'Hadrian's Column of Trajan' *Journal of Roman Archaeology* 6, 5–22

Claridge, A. 1998 *Rome. An Oxford Archaeological Guide.* Oxford University Press, Oxford

Claridge, A. 2005 'Further Considerations on the Carving of the Frieze on the Column of Marcus Aurelius' *Journal of Roman Archaeology* 18 Fasc. 1, 313–316

Clarke, D. 2005 *The Angel of Mons. Phantom Soldiers and Ghostly Guardians.* Wiley, Chichester

Coarelli, F. 2000 *The Column of Trajan.* Editore Colombo, Rome

Coleman, K.M. 1990 'Fatal Charades: Roman Executions Staged as Mythological Enactments' *Journal of Roman Studies* 80, 44–73

Coleman, K.M. 1998 'The Contagion of the Throng: Absorbing Violence in the Roman World' *Hermathena* 164, 65–88

Colini, A.M. 1954 *Piazza Colonna. Mostre topografiche di Roma, Palazzo Braschi Dicembre 1954–Gennaio 1955.* Comune di Roma, Rome

Colini, A.M. 1955 'Vicende della Colonna dall'antichità ai nostri giorni' in Caprino *et al.* 1955, 31–42

Condurachi, E. (ed.) 1982 *L'esame storico-artistico della Colonna Traina.* Colloquio Italo-
Romano, Accademia Nazionale dei Lincei, Rome

Corbeill, A. 2004 *Nature Embodied: Gesture in Ancient Rome.* Princeton University Press,
Princeton, New Jersey

Coulston, J.C.N. 1990 'The Architecture and Construction Scenes on Trajan's Column'
in Henig, M. (ed.) 1990 *Architecture and Architectural Sculpture in the Roman Empire.*
Oxford University Committee for Archaeology Monograph 29, 39–50. Oxford

Coulston, J.C.N. 2009 *All the Emperor's Men: Roman Soldiers and Barbarians on Trajan's
Column.* Oxbow Books, Oxford

Cunliffe, B.W. and Fulford, M.G. 1982 'Bath and the Rest of Wessex' *Corpus Signorum
Imperii Romani vol.* 1 Fascicule 2. British Academy

D'Ambra, E. 1993 *Private Lives, Imperial Virtues. The Frieze of the Forum Transitorium in
Rome.* Princeton University Press, Princeton

David, J-M. 2000 'Les Contiones Militaires des Colonnes Trajane et Aurélienne: les
Nécessités de l'Adhésion' in Scheid, J. and Huet, V. (eds) 2000, 213–226

Davies, P.J.E. 2000 *Death and the Emperor. Roman Imperial Funerary Monuments from
Augustus to Marcus Aurelius.* Cambridge University Press, Cambridge

Dillon, S. 2006 'Women on the Columns of Trajan and Marcus Aurelius and the Visual
Language of Roman Victory' in Dillon, S. and Welch, K.E. (eds) 2006, 244–271

Dillon, S. and Welch, K.E. (eds) 2006 *Representations of War in Ancient Rome.* Cambridge
University Press, Cambridge

Dobias, J. 1932 'Le Monnayage de l'Empereur Marc-Aurèle et les Bas-Reliefs
Historiques Contemporains' *Revue Numismatiques* 4.35, 127–161

Dodd, C.H. 1913 'Chronology of the Danubian Wars of the Emperor Marcus Aurelius'
Numismatic Chronicle Fourth Series 13, 162–199

Dubois, P. 1996 'Archaic Bodies in Pieces' in Kampen, N.B. (ed.) 1996, 55–64

Durnan, N. 2000 'Stone Sculpture' in Ling, R. (ed.) 2000 *Making Classical Art. Process and
Practice,* 18–36. Tempus, Stroud

Elsner, J. 2000 'Frontality in the Column of Marcus Aurelius' in Scheid, J. and Huet, V.
(eds) 2000, 251–264

Farquharson, A.S.L. 1951 *Marcus Aurelius. His Life and his World.* Greenwood Press, Westport

Fears, J.R. 1981 'Jupiter and Roman Imperial Ideology' *Aufstieg und Niedergang der
Römischen Welt* 2.17.1, 3–141

Fears, R. 1981 'The Cult of Virtues and Roman Imperial Ideology' *Aufstieg und
Niedergang der Römischen Welt* II.17.2, 827–948

Feinstein, W. 2003 *The Civilization of the Holocaust in Italy: Poets, Artists, Saints, Anti-
Semites.* Fairleigh Dickinson University Press, Madison

Ferguson, J. 1980 *The Arts in Britain in World War I.* Stainer and Bell, London

Ferris, I.M. 1994 'Insignificant Others; Images of Barbarians on Military Art from
Roman Britain' in Cottam, S., Dungworth, D., Scott, S. and Taylor, J. (eds) 1994
*TRAC 94. Proceedings of the Fourth Annual Theoretical Roman Archaeology Conference,
Durham 1994,* 24–31. Oxbow Books, Oxford

Ferris, I.M. 1997 'The Enemy Without, the Enemy Within: More Thoughts on Images of
Barbarians in Greek and Roman Art' in Meadows, K., Lemke, C., and Heron, J (eds)
1997 *TRAC 96. Proceedings of the Sixth Annual Theoretical Roman Archaeology Conference
Sheffield 1996,* 22–28. Oxbow Books, Oxford

Ferris, I.M. 2000 *Enemies of Rome. Barbarians Through Roman Eyes*. Sutton Publishing,
      Stroud
Ferris, I.M. 2001 'The Body Politic: the Sexuality of Barbarians in Augustan Art' in
      Bevan, L. (ed.) 2001 *Indecent Exposure. Sexuality, Society and the Archaeological Record*,
      100–109. Cruithne Press, Glasgow
Ferris, I.M. 2002 'A Note on a Bronze Figurine of a Barbarian Captive from Northern
      England'. *Durham Archaeological Journal* 16, 19–20
Ferris, I.M. 2003a 'The Hanged Men Dance. Barbarians in Trajanic Art' in Scott, S. and
      Webster, J. (eds) 2003, 53–68
Ferris, I.M. 2003b 'An Empire in Pieces. Considering the Fragment in Roman Art and
      Archaeology' in Carr, G., Swift, E. and Weekes, J. (eds) 2003 *TRAC 2002: Proceedings of
      the Twelfth Theoretical Roman Archaeology Conference, Canterbury, 14–28.* Oxbow Books,
      Oxford
Ferris, I.M. 2006 'Suffering in Silence. The Political Aesthetics of Pain in Antonine Art'
      in Pollard, T. and Banks, I. (eds) *Past Tense. Studies in the Archaeology of Conflict*, 67–92.
      Brill, Leiden
Ferris, I.M. 2007 'A Severed Head. Prolegomena to a Study of the Fragmented Body in
      Roman Art and Archaeology' in Hingley, R. and Willis, S. (eds) 2007 *Roman Finds:
      Context and Theory*, 115–126. Oxbow Books, Oxford
Foss, C. 1990 *Roman Historical Coins*. Seaby, London
Fowden, G. 1987 'Pagan Versions of the Rain Miracle of AD 172' *Historia* 36, 83–95
Fredrick, D. (ed.) 2002 *The Roman Gaze. Vision, Power, and the Body*. Johns Hopkins
      University Press, Baltimore
Fuhrmann, H. 1937 'Ein Fragment des Verlorene Reliefs am Sockel der Marcussäule'
      Mitteilungen des Deutschen Archäologischen Instituts, Römische Abteilungen 52, 261–265
Futrell, A. 1997 *Blood in the Arena*. University of Texas Press, Austin
Galinier, M. 2000 'La Colonne de Marc Aurèle: Réflexion sur une Gestuelle Narrative'
      in Scheid, J. and Huet, V. (eds) 2000, 141–162
Gatti, G. 1955 'La *Columna Divi Marci* nelle sue caratteristiche architettoniche e nel suo
      ambiente' in Caprino *et al.* 1955, 15–28
Gergel, R.A. 1994 'Costume as Geographical Indicator: Barbarians and Prisoners on
      Cuirassed Statue Breastplates' in Sebesta, J.J. and Bonfante, L. (eds) 1994 *The World of
      Roman Costume*, 191–212. University of Wisconsin Press, Madison
Gilliver, K. 1995 'The Roman Army and Morality in War' in Lloyd, A. (ed.) 1995 *Battle in
      Antiquity*, 219–238. Duckworth, London
Goldsworthy, A. 1996 *The Roman Army at War 100 BC to AD 200*. Oxford University Press,
      Oxford
Gore, F. 1987 'The Resilient Figures: Mark Gertler and Matthew Smith' in Compton, S.
      (ed.) 1987 *British Art in the 20ᵗʰ Century*, 172–185. Royal Academy of Arts, London
Görlitz, W. 1954 *Marc Aurel. Kaiser und Philosoph*. Kohlhammer, Stuttgart
Goulaki-Voutira, A. 1992 'Nike' in *Lexikon Iconographicum Mythologiae Classicae* 6, 859–881
Graf, F. 2000 'Versuch Einer Forschungsgeschichte' in Scheid, J. and Huet, V. (eds) 2000,
      133–140
Green, M. 1991 *The Sun-Gods of Ancient Europe*. Batsford, London
Gregory, A.P. 1994 ''Powerful Images': Responses to Portraits and the Political Uses of
      Images in Rome' *Journal of Roman Archaeology* 7, 80–99

Grimal, P. 1991 *Marc Aurèle.* Fayard, Paris

Guey, J. 1948a 'La Date de la 'Pluie Miracleuse' (172 Après J.C.) et la Colonne Aurélienne' *Mélanges d'Archéologie et d'Histoire* 60, 105–127

Guey, J. 1948b 'Encore la 'Pluie Miracleuse'' *Revue de Philologie* 22, 16–62

Guey, J. 1949 'La Date de la 'Pluie Miracleuse' (172 Apres J.C.) et la Colonne Aurelienne II' *Melanges d'Archeologie et d'Histoire* 61, 93–118

Hamberg, P.G. 1945 *Studies in Roman Imperial Art.* Almquist and Wiksell Boktryckeri Aktiebolag, Uppsala

Hannestad, N. 1988 *Roman Art and Imperial Policy.* Aarhus University Press, Aarhus

Hannestad, N. 2001 'Rome and Her Enemies. Warfare in Roman Imperial Art' in Bekker-Nielsen, T. and Hannestad, L. (eds) 2001 *War as a Cultural and Social Force*, 146–154. Historisk-filosofiske Skrifter 22, Copenhagen

Hanoune, R. 2000 'Représentations de Construction et d'Architecture sur la Colonne Aurélienne' in Scheid, J. and Huet, V. (eds) 2000, 205–212

Harris, W.V. 2005 'Can Enemies Too Be Brave? A Question about Roman Representation of the Other' in Petraccia, M.F. (ed.) *Il Cittadino, lo Straniero, il Barbaro, fra Integrazione ed Emarginazione nell'Antichita*, 465–472. G. Bretschneider, Rome

Hassall, M.W.C. 1977 'Wingless Victories' in Munby, J. and Henig, M. (eds) 1977 *Roman Life and Art in Britain.* BAR British Series 41, 327–340. Oxford

Häussler, R. 1999 'Performance and Ritual: the Role of State Architecture in the Roman Empire' in Baker, P. *et al.* (eds) 1999, 1–13

Hölscher, T. 2000 'Die Säule des Marcus Aurelius: Narrative Struktur und Ideologische Botschaft' in Scheid, J. and Huet, V. (eds) 2000, 89–105

Hölscher, T. 2000 'Images of War in Greece and Rome' *Journal of Roman Studies* 93, 1–17

Hölscher, T. 1967 *Victoria Romana Archäologische Untersuchungen zur Geschichte und Wesenart der Römischen Siegesgöttin von den Anfängen bis zum Ende der 3. Jhrs n. Chr.* Philipp von Zabern, Mainz

Hölscher, T. 2006 'The Transformation of Victory into Power: from Event to Structure' in Dillon, S. and Welch, K.E. (eds) 2006, 27–48

Hopkins, K. 1983 'Murderous Games' in Hopkins, K. (ed.) 1983 *Death and Renewal: Sociological Studies in Roman History* vol. *2,* 120–123. Cambridge University Press, Cambridge

Huet, V. 1996 'Stories One Might tell of Roman Art' in Elsner, J. (ed.) 1996 *Art and Text in Roman Culture*, 8–31. Cambridge University Press, Cambridge

Huet, V. 2000 'Historiographie des Études sur la Colonne Aurélienne' in Scheid, J. and Huet, V. (eds) 2000, 107–132

Israelowich, I. 2008 'The Rain Miracle of Marcus Aurelius. (Re-) Construction of Concensus' *Greece and Rome* vol. 55 No. 1, 83–102

James, S. 1999 'The Community of the Soldiers: a Major Identity and Centre of Power in the Roman Empire' in Baker, P. *et al.* (eds) 1999, 14–25

James, S. 2002 'Writing the Legions: the Development and Future of Roman Military Studies in Britain' *Archaeological Journal* vol. 159, 1–58

James, S. Forthcoming Roman Violence

Jobst, W. 1978 *11. Juni 172 N. CHR. Der Tag des Blitz-und Regenwunders im Quadenlande.* Verlag der Österreichischen Akademie der Wissenschaften, Philosophisch-Histoische Klasse Sitzungsberichte, 335, Vienna

Jolivet,V. 1988 'Les Cendres d'Auguste. Note sur la Topographie Monumentale du Champ de Mars Septentrionale' *Archeologia Laziale* 9, 90–96

Jordan-Ruwe, M. 1990 'Zur Rekonstruktion und Datierung der Marcussäule' *Boreas* 13, 53–69

Kampen, N.B. 1981 'Biographical Narration and Roman Funerary Art' *American Journal of Archaeology* 85, 47–58

Kampen, N.B. 1991a 'Between Public and Private: Women as Historical Subjects in Roman Art' in Pomeroy, S.B. (ed.) 1991 *Women's History and Ancient History*, 218–248. University of North Carolina Press, Chapel Hill

Kampen, N.B. 1991b 'Reliefs of the Basilica Aemilia' *Klio: Beitrage zur Alten Geschichte* 73, 448–458

Kampen, N.B. 1995 'Looking at Gender: the Column of Trajan and Roman Historical Reliefs' in Stanton, D.C. and Stewart, A.J. (eds) 1995 *Feminisms in the Academy*, 46–73. University of Michigan Press, Ann Arbor

Kampen, N.B. (ed.) 1996 *Sexuality in Ancient Art*. Cambridge University Press, Cambridge

Kellum, B. 1996 'The Phallus as Signifier: the Forum of Augustus and Rituals of Masculinity' in Boymel Kampen, N. (ed.) 1996 *Sexuality in Ancient Art,* 170–183. Cambridge University Press, Cambridge

Kerr, W.G. 1995 *A Chronological Study of the Marcomannic Wars of Marcus Aurelius.* Princeton University Press, Princeton, New Jersey

Klein, R. (ed.) 1979 *Marc Aurel*. Wissenschaftliche Buchgesellschaft, Darmstadt

Klein, R. 1991 'Das Regenwunder im Quadenland' in Habelt, R. (ed.) 1991 *Bonner Historia Augusta Colloquium,* 117–138

Kleiner, D.E.E. 1981 'Second-Century Mythological Portraits: Mars and Venus' *Latomus,* 512–544

Kleiner, D.E.E. 1992 *Roman Sculpture*. Yale University Press, Yale

Kleiner, F.S. 1991 'The Trophy on the Bridge and the Roman Triumph over Nature' *L'Antiquité Classique* 60, 182–192

Koeppel, G. 2002 'The Column of Trajan: Narrative Technique and the Image of the Emperor' in Stadter, P.A. and Van der Stockt, L. (eds) 2002 *Sage and Emperor: Plutarch, Greek Intellectuals, and Roman Power in the Time of Trajan (98–117 AD)*, 245–257. Leuven University Press, Leuven

Kohne, E. and Ewigleben, C. (eds) 2000 *Gladiators and Caesars. The Power of Spectacle in Ancient Rome*. British Museum Press, London

Kousser, R. 2006 'Conquest and Desire: Roman Victoria in Public and Provincial Sculpture' in Dillon, S. and Welch, K.E. (eds) 2006, 218–243

Kousser, R. 2008 *Hellenistic and Roman Ideal Sculpture. The Allure of the Classical.* Cambridge University Press, Cambridge

Kristeva, J. 1998 *Visions Capitales.* Réunion des Musées Nationaux, Paris

Kunze, M. 1992 *Le Grand Autel de Marbre de Pergame. Redécouverte, Historique et Reconstruction.* Staatliche Museen zu Berlin. Verlag Philipp von Zabern, Mainz

Kyle, D.G. 1998 *Spectacles of Death in Ancient Rome.* Routledge, London

La Rocca, E. 1986 *Rilievi storici Capitolini: Il restauro dei Pannelli di Adriano e di Marco Aurelio nel Palazzo dei Conservatori.* De Luca, Rome

Lepper, F. and Frere, S.S. 1988 *Trajan's Column*. Alan Sutton, Gloucester

Levi, A.C. 1952 *Barbarians on Roman Imperial Coins and Sculpture*. American Numismatic Society Numismatic Notes and Monographs No.123

Lintott, A.W. 1968 *Violence in Republican Rome*. Clarendon Press, Oxford

MacMullen, R. 1986 'Judicial Savagery in the Roman Empire' Reprinted in MacMullen, R. 1990 *Changes in the Roman Empire. Essays in the Ordinary, 204–217*. Princeton University Press, Princeton, New Jersey

Maffei, S. 1990 'La '*Felicitas Imperatoris*' e il dominio sugli elementi' *Studi Classici e Orientali* 40, 329–367

Maffei, S. 1993 *Colonna Marci Aurelii Antonini*. Lexicon Topographicum Urbis Romae

Maffei, S. 1996 'Colonna di Marco Aurelio' *Enciclopedia dell'Arte Antica, Classica e Orientale,* 234–237

Martines, G. 2000 'L'Architettura' in Scheid, J. and Huet, V. (eds) 2000, 19–88

Morris, J. 1952 'The Dating of the Column of Marcus Aurelius' *Journal of the Warburg and Courtauld Institutes* 15, 33–43

Mulvey, L. 1975 'Visual Pleasure and Narrative Cinema' *Screen* 16.6–18

Mulvey, L. 1989 *Visual and Other Pleasures*. Indiana University Press, Bloomington

Ostrowski, J.A. 1990 'Personifications of Rivers as an Element of Roman Political Propaganda' *Études et Travaux. Studia I Prace. Travaux du Centre d'Archéologie Méditerranéen de l'Académie des Sciences Polonaise* 15, 309–315

Packer, J.E. 1997 *The Forum of Trajan in Rome: a Study of the Monument*. Vols 1–3. University of California Press, Berkeley

Panzanelli, R. (ed.) 2008 *The Color of Life: Polychromy in Sculpture from Antiquity to the Present*. J. Paul Getty Museum, Los Angeles

Petersen, E., von Domaszewski, A., and Calderini, G. 1896 *Die Marcus-Säule auf Piazza Colonna in Rom*. F. Bruckmann a.g., Munich

Pirson, F. 1996 'Style and Message on the Column of Marcus Aurelius' *Papers of the British School at Rome* 64, 139–179

Plass, P. 1995 *The Game of Death in Ancient Rome*. University of Wisconsin Press, Madison

Potter, D.S. and Mattingly, D.J. (eds) 1998 *Life, Death and Entertainment in the Roman Empire*. University of Michigan Press, Ann Arbor

Rawson, P.B. 1987 *The Myth of Marsyas in the Roman Visual Arts: an Iconographic Study*. BAR International Series 347. BAR, Oxford

Renan, E. 1923 'Marc-Aurèle et la Fin du Monde Antique' in *Histoire des origines du Christianisme,* 24th edition. Calmann-Levy, Paris

Rich, J. and Shipley, G. (eds) 1993 *War and Society in the Roman World*. Routledge, London

Richmond, I.A. 1982 *Trajan's Army on Trajan's Column*. Reprint. British School at Rome, Rome

Robert, R. 2000 'Ambiguité de la Gestuelle 'Pathétique' sur la Colonne Aurélienne' in Scheid, J. and Huet, V. (eds) 2000, 175–196

Rodgers, R. 2003 'Female Representation in Roman Art: Feminising the Provincial 'Other'' in Scott, S. and Webster, J. (eds) 2003, 69–94

Roos, A.G. 1943 *Het Regenwonder op de Zuil Can Marcus Aurelius*. Noord Hollandsche Uitgerers Maatschappij, Amsterdam

Rosen, K. 1997 *Marc Aurel*. Rowohlt, Hamburg

Rossi, L. 1971 *Trajan's Column and the Dacian Wars*. Thames and Hudson, London

Rossi, L. 1978 'Technique, Toil and Triumph on the Danube in Trajan's Propaganda Programme' *Antiquaries Journal* 58, 81–87

Rossi, L. 1981 *Rotocalchi di pietra: segni e disegni dei tempi sui monumenti trionfali dell'impero Romano.* Jacabook, Milan

Rubin, H.Z. 1979 'Weather Miracles Under Marcus Aurelius' *Athenaeum* 75, 357–380

Ryberg, I.S. 1955 *Rites of the State Religion in Roman Art.* Memoirs of the American Academy at Rome 22

Ryberg, I.S. 1967 *Panel Reliefs of Marcus Aurelius.* Archaeological Institute of America, New York

Sage, M.M. 1987 'Eusebius and the Rain Miracle. Some Observations' *Historia* 36, 96–113

Sakowski, A. 1988 'Die Marc Aurel-Säule und die Markomannenkriege' in Stemmer, K. (ed.) 1988, 108–116

Sauron, G. 2000 'Une Innovation du Symbolisme Gestuel sur la Colonne Aurélienne: la 'Convention Optique'' in Scheid, J. and Huet, V. (eds) 2000, 245–250

Schall, U. 1991 *Marc Aurel. Der Philosoph auf dem Caesarenthron.* Esslingen, Munich

Scheid, J. 2000 'Sujets Religieux et Gestes Rituels sur la Colonne Aurélienne. Questions sur la Religion à l'Époque de Marc Aurèle' in Scheid, J. and Huet, V. (eds) 2000, 227–244

Scheid, J. and Huet, V. (eds) 2000 *Autour de la Colonne Aurélienne. Geste e Image sur la Colonne de Marc Aurèle à Rome.* Brepols, Turnhout

Settis, S. 1985 'La Colonne Trajane. Invention, Composition, Disposition' *Annales, économies, sociétés, civilisations* 40, 1151–1194

Settis, S. 1988 *La Colonna Traina.* Einaudi, Turin

Sommella, A.M. (ed.) 1990 *The Equestrian Statue of Marcus Aurelius in Campidoglio.* Silvana Editoriale, Rome

Sommella, A.M. and Presicce, C.P. (eds) 1997 *Il Marco Aurelio e la sua copia.* Silvana Editoriale, Rome

Spivey, N. 2001 *Enduring Creation: Art, Pain and Fortitude.* Thames and Hudson, London

Stemmer, K. (ed.) 1988 *Kaiser Marc Aurel und Seine Zeit.* Abguss-Sammlung Antiker Plastik, Berlin

Stewart, P. 2003 *Statues in Roman Society. Representation and Response.* Oxford University Press, Oxford

Strong, D.E. 1961 *Roman Imperial Sculpture. An Introduction to the Commemorative and Decorative Sculpture of the Roman Empire Down to the Death of Constantine.* Alec Tiranti, London

Timonen, A. 2000 *Cruelty and Death. Roman Historians' Scenes of Imperial Violence from Commodus to Philippus Arabus* Annales Universitatis Turkuensis, Ser. B Humaniors 241, Turku, Finland

Uzzi, J.D. 2005 *Children in the Visual Arts of Imperial Rome.* Cambridge University Press, Cambridge

Visser, R. 1992 'Fascist Doctrine and the Cult of the Romanità' *Journal of Contemporary History,* vol. 27 No. 1, 5–22

Vogel, L. 1973 *The Column of Antoninus Pius.* Harvard University Press, Cambridge Mass

Voisin, J.L. 1982 'Les Romains, Chasseurs de Têtes' in *Du Châtiment dans la Cité. Supplices Corporels et Peine de Mort dans le Monde Antique.* Atti del Congresso, Roma 1984, 241–292

Von Domaszewski, A. 1909 'Die Triumphstrasse auf dem Marsfelde' *Archiv fur Religionswissenschaft* 12, 70–73

Vout, C. 2007 *Power and Eroticism in Imperial Rome.* Cambridge University Press, Cambridge

Vulpe, R. 1973 'Prigonieri Romani suppliziati da donne Dacie sul rilievo della Colonna Traiana' *Rivista Storica dell'Antichità* 3, 109–125

Walter, H. 1984 *La Porte Noire de Besançon. Contribution a l'Étude de l'Art Triomphal des Gaules* Centre de Recherches d'Histoire Ancienne vol. 65. Annales Littéraires de l'Universitée de Besançon

Walter, H. 1993 *Les Barbares de l'Occident Romain. Corpus des Gaules et des Provinces de Germanie.* Centre de Recherches d'Histoire Ancienne vol. 122. Annales Littéraires de l'Université de Besançon

Webster, J. 1997 'A Negotiated Syncretism: Readings on the Development of Romano-Celtic Religion' in Mattingly, D.J. (ed.) 1997 *Dialogues in Roman Imperialism. Power, Discourse, and Discrepant Experience in the Roman Empire.* Journal of Roman Archaeology Supplementary Series No. 23, 165–184

Wegner, M. 1931 'Die Kunstgeschichtliche Stellung der Markussäaule' *Jahrbuch des Deutschen Archäologischen Instituts* 46, 61–174

Wegner, M. 1938 'Bemerkungen zu den Ehrendenkmalern des Marcus Aurelius' *Archäologischer Anzeiger* 53, 157–195

Weis, A. 1992 *The Hanging Marsyas and its Copies: Roman Innovations in a Hellenistic Sculptural Tradition.* G. Bretschneider, Rome

Wiedemann, T. 1992 *Emperors and Gladiators.* Routledge, London

Wilson-Jones, M. 1993 'One Hundred Feet and a Spiral Stair: the Problem of Designing Trajan's Column' *Journal of Roman Archaeology* 6, 23–38

Wolff, H. 1994 'Die Markus-Säule als Quelle fur die Markomannenkreige' in Friesenger, H., Tejral, J. and Stuppner, A. (eds) 1994 *Markomannenkreig. Ursachen und Wirkungen,* Brno, 73–84

Wyss, E. 1996 *The Myth of Apollo and Marsyas in the Art of the Italian Renaissance: an Inquiry into the Meaning of Images.* University of Delaware Press, Newark

Zanker, P. 1998 'Die Barbaren, der Kaiser und die Arena. Bilder der Gewalt in der Römischen Kunst' reprinted in translation as 'I Barbari, l'Imperatore e l'Arena. Immagini di Violenza nell'arte Romana' in Zanker, P. 2002 *Un'arte per l'impero. Funzione e intenzione delle immagini nel mondo Romano, 38–62.* Electa, Milan

Zanker, P. 2000 'Die Frauen und Kinder der Barbaren auf der Markussäule' in Scheid, J. and Huet (eds) 2000, 163–174

Zwikker, W. 1941 *Studien zur Marcussäule.* PhD dissertation, University of Amsterdam

Index

As the principal subject of this book is the Column of Marcus Aurelius, Marcus's life, and the barbarian peoples against whom he fought his wars, these three topics have not been included in this index, given that otherwise each would appear hundreds of times.